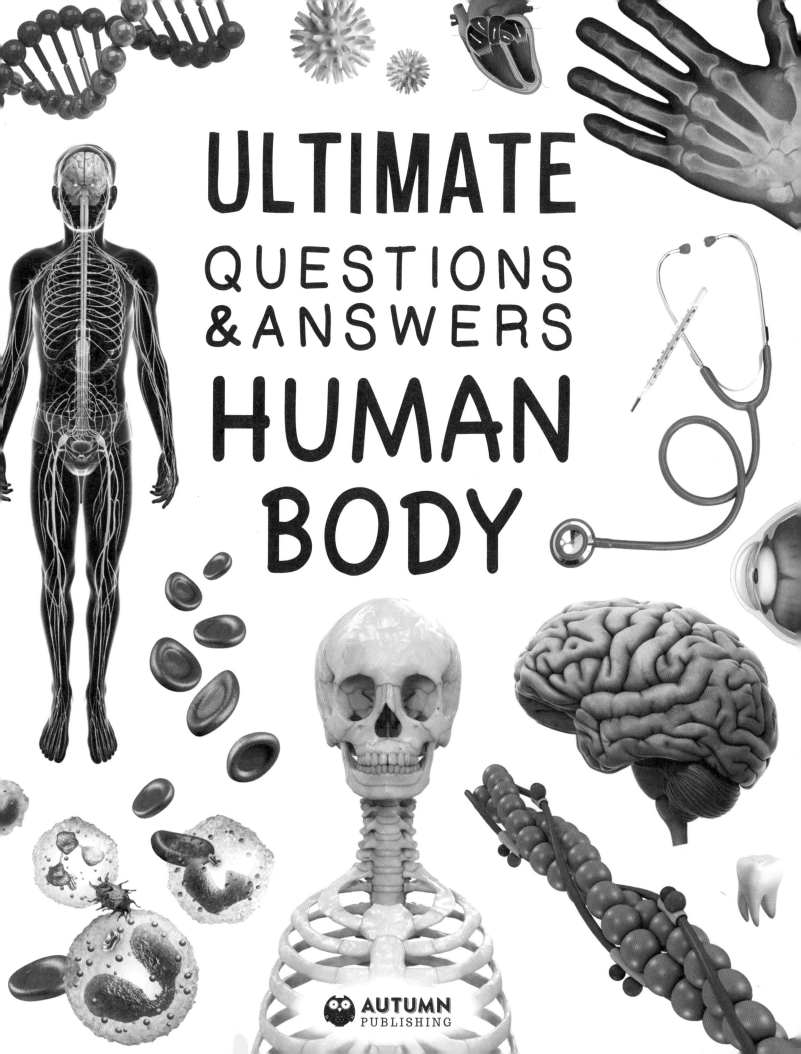

ULTIMATE QUESTIONS & ANSWERS HUMAN BODY

AUTUMN PUBLISHING

CONTENTS

HOW WE WORK...4

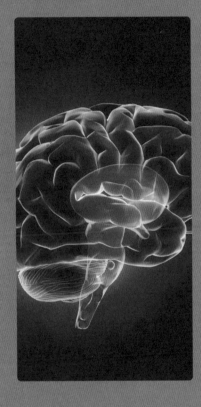
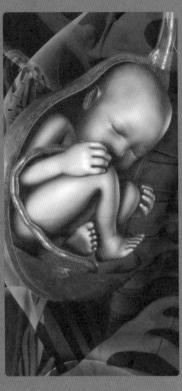

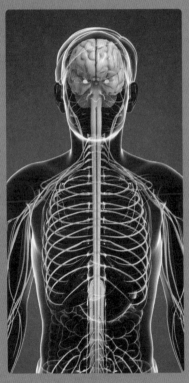

BONES AND MUSCLES...26

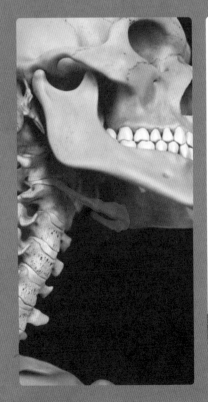
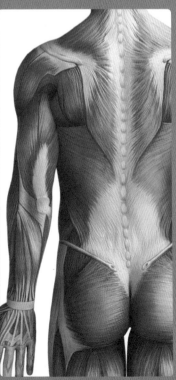
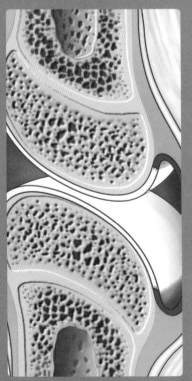
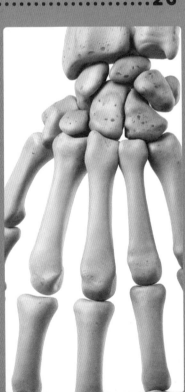

COMMUNICATION AND THE SENSES 32

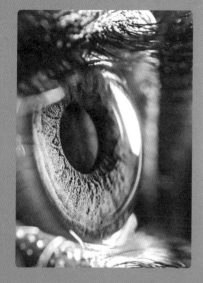
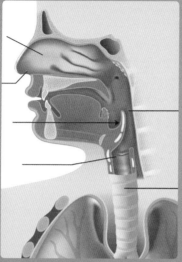

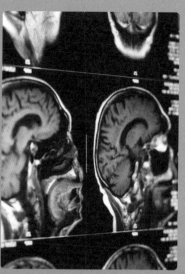

A HEALTHY BODY 44

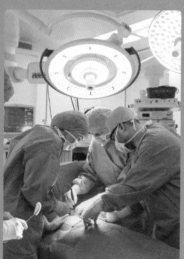

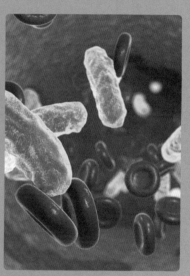

DIET 58

WHAT IS A GENE?

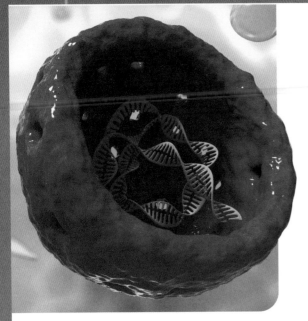

Nucleus of a human cell showing DNA

Inside the nucleus of every human cell are chromosomes. These are made up of material called DNA, which consists of genes. Each gene is one set of instructions to the cell to make different proteins. Basically, the instructions in our genes decide all of our physical features, such as height and color of the eyes. Imagine the cell is a computer and the DNA or genes are the software that runs in it.

WHY IS THE STUDY OF GENES SO IMPORTANT?

Knowing how our genes act helps scientists understand how the body works. They can figure out our chances of getting a certain disease, how good we could be at a sport, or why one person's memory is sharper than the next person's. The study of genes also helps in tracing our histories and ancestors.

Analyzing samples

Big? ARE GENES AND GENOMES THE SAME?

DNA test showing genome sequencing

A gene is one set of instructions to a cell. A genome is a complete set of a human's instructions—their DNA, including all the genes in it—there are about 20,500 human genes in all. Every single genome has all of the information needed to build and keep a person's body functioning. But the different types of cells in the body interpret the same information coded in the DNA differently while performing their specialized functions.

Inheriting features from our parents

HOW DO WE GET OUR GENES?

We inherit our genes from our parents—half from our mom and half from our dad. So the gene containing instructions for one feature of your body—for example, the eyes—will have two versions. One could be for blue eyes (your mother) and one for brown eyes (your father). The gene that is the dominant one of the two will decide which color your eyes will be.

CAN GENES AFFECT OUR HEALTH?

Checking why you're feeling sick

Sometimes a gene may carry instructions that are slightly different from those carried in the usual version of the same gene. This is called a variant gene. If the protein made by the cell according to the variant gene's instructions affects an important function of the body, it can make us become sick.

CAN HUMAN GENES BE ALTERED?

Yes, this is called gene editing or genetic engineering. It is done by changing the genetic material of the cells either to stop a problem-causing gene, or to fix it by replacing it with healthy material.

Genetic engineering

Rapid-FIRE ?

HOW MANY GENES DECIDE THE COLOR OF OUR SKIN?

More than 150!

Genes make the difference

WHAT DOES DNA LOOK LIKE?

Like a twisted ladder.

DNA

HOW MANY CHROMOSOMES DO HUMANS HAVE?

23 pairs.

WHAT DOES THE BRAIN DO?

Our brain controls the body, keeping the vital organs working, and collecting information from the senses so that we can feel, taste, hear, smell, and see. At the same time, it sends messages to the muscles to react to situations. The brain also controls everything we think and feel, as well as storing memories of the past.

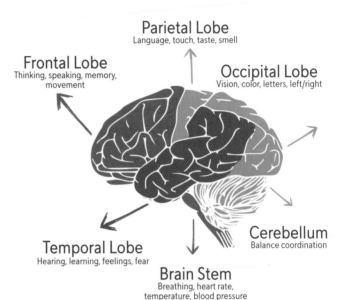

Parietal Lobe
Language, touch, taste, smell

Frontal Lobe
Thinking, speaking, memory, movement

Occipital Lobe
Vision, color, letters, left/right

Temporal Lobe
Hearing, learning, feelings, fear

Brain Stem
Breathing, heart rate, temperature, blood pressure

Cerebellum
Balance coordination

Functions of the brain

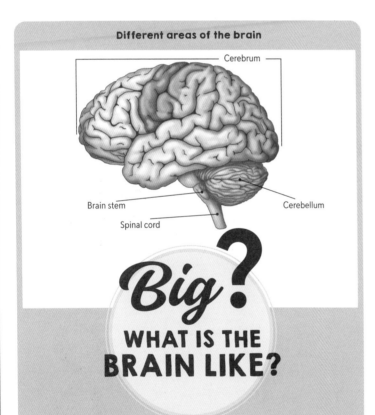

Different areas of the brain

Cerebrum

Brain stem

Cerebellum

Spinal cord

Big? WHAT IS THE BRAIN LIKE?

Inside our head is the most amazingly complex known structure in the Universe: the human brain. It looks like a huge, soggy gray walnut with a wrinkled surface. But within this mass are billions of intricately interconnected nerve cells. The chemical and electrical impulses continually shooting through our brain cells produce all our thoughts, record every sensation, and control nearly all our actions by linking to the whole body through a network of nerves.

WHAT IS THE DIFFERENCE BETWEEN THE RIGHT AND LEFT BRAIN?

The brain is divided into two hemispheres or halves. It is widely believed that people who are more creative and artistic use the right hemisphere more, and those who think logically and methodically use the brain's left hemisphere more.

Left and right brain

WHAT HAPPENS IN THE CORE OF THE BRAIN?

The core of the brain includes the thalamus and midbrain and controls basic functions such as breathing and heart rate, without our awareness. The hypothalamus is also here and controls hunger and sleeping. Around the thalamus is the limbic system, which controls a lot of our behavior.

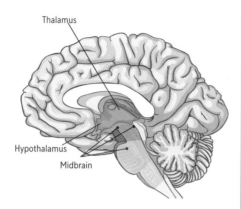

Thalamus

Hypothalamus

Midbrain

The core of the brain

WHERE DOES THINKING TAKE PLACE?

The cerebrum

In the cerebrum, the huge wrinkled part that wraps around the core of the brain. The cerebrum is where we think and where complex tasks such as memory, speech, and control of movement take place. All the folds of the cerebrum allow a huge number of nerve cells to be squeezed inside the skull.

HOW DOES A BRAIN SCAN HELP SCIENTISTS?

Brain scans are made with special machines. The scanned image shows doctors and scientists what is going on inside a living brain. With the help of this tool, scientists have gotten to know a great deal about how the brain works. For example, it is now possible to identify which areas of the brain are active when we are speaking.

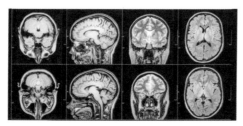

Brain scans

Rapid-FIRE ?

HOW MUCH DOES THE BRAIN WEIGH?

On average, about 3.3 pounds.

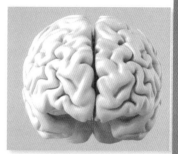

Two halves of the brain

WHERE ARE HUNGER AND THIRST CONTROLLED?

In the hypothalamus. Body temperature is also controlled here.

Quenching thirst

WHAT DOES THE BRAIN STEM DO?

It regulates our heart rate and breathing.

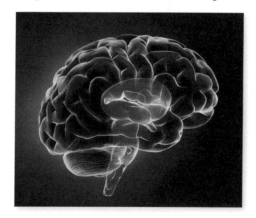

The brain stem

WHICH PART OF THE BRAIN RECOGNIZES COLORS?

The cortex.

WHAT IS BLOOD?

Blood is a mix of red blood cells, white blood cells, and platelets in a clear, yellowish fluid called plasma. Salts, hormones, fats, and sugar are also present in the plasma. Hemoglobin in the red blood cells is rich in iron and gives blood its bright red color.

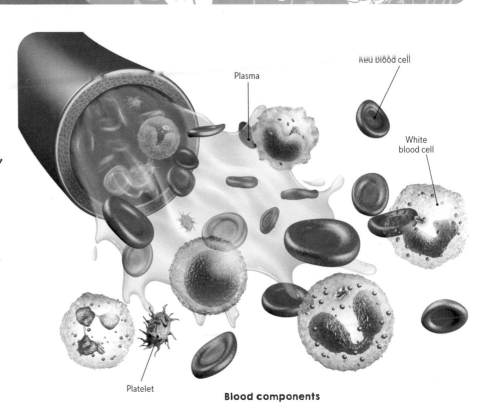

Plasma

Red blood cell

White blood cell

Platelet

Blood components

HOW OFTEN DOES THE HEART BEAT?

A child's heart usually beats about 80 times a minute, which is a bit faster than an adult's. An adult heart beats 70 times a minute. During running or vigorous exercise the heart beats much faster.

Big ?

WHAT IS THE CARDIOVASCULAR SYSTEM?

It is a vast network of organs and blood vessels that keeps us alive and healthy. This system is responsible for circulating blood, which contains vital nutrients, to all parts of the body. It also acts as the waste removal system. While delivering nutrients, oxygen, and hormones to each cell, waste products such as carbon dioxide are removed, keeping our cells healthy. The central organ of the cardiovascular system is the heart. The heart pumps blood around the body constantly. Blood is pumped out from the heart through blood vessels called arteries, and back into the heart through veins.

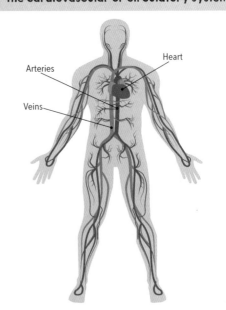

The cardiovascular or circulatory system

Heart

Arteries

Veins

HOW DOES THE **HEART PUMP?**

The heart is not just one pump but two, separated by a thick wall of muscle called the septum. Blood from the veins flows into each half of the heart from the top, flooding the atrium, the first of the two chambers. This is a small reservoir where blood builds up before entering the second chamber, or ventricle. The ventricle squeezes the blood out and sends it shooting through the arteries.

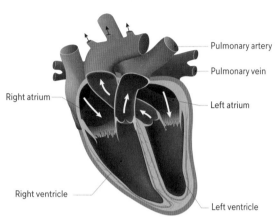

Pulmonary artery

Pulmonary vein

Right atrium

Left atrium

Left ventricle

Right ventricle

Parts of the heart

WHAT IS A **CAPILLARY?**

Blood travels around the body through tubes called arteries and veins. These branch off into smaller tubes that reach every cell of the body. Capillaries are the tiniest blood vessels of all. Most capillaries are thinner than a single hair.

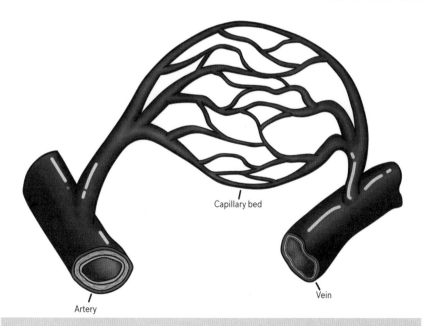

Capillary bed

Artery

Vein

Capillaries

Rapid-FIRE ?

HOW **MANY CELLS ARE THERE IN ONE DROP OF BLOOD?**

Up to five million red blood cells!

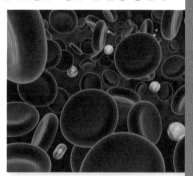

Tightly packed red blood cells

WHAT IS THE **PULSE?**

The shock waves that circulate due to the pumping of the heart. They can be detected on the inside of the wrist, and some other points on the body.

Feeling the pulse

IS THE **HEART EXACTLY IN THE MIDDLE OF THE CHEST?**

No, its centerline is slightly to the left of the breastbone.

Position of the heart

HOW LARGE IS THE **NETWORK OF BLOOD VESSELS?**

More than 62,000 miles in a human body—they could circle the globe at least twice!

WHAT DOES **PULSE RATE INDICATE?**

Counting the number of pulses tells us how fast the heart is beating.

WHAT ARE THE KIDNEYS?

The kidneys are two bean-shaped organs in the middle of the back. As they filter blood, they regulate body fluids and salt levels and control acid levels in the blood. They filter approximately seven quarts of blood an hour.

The kidneys—from outside and inside

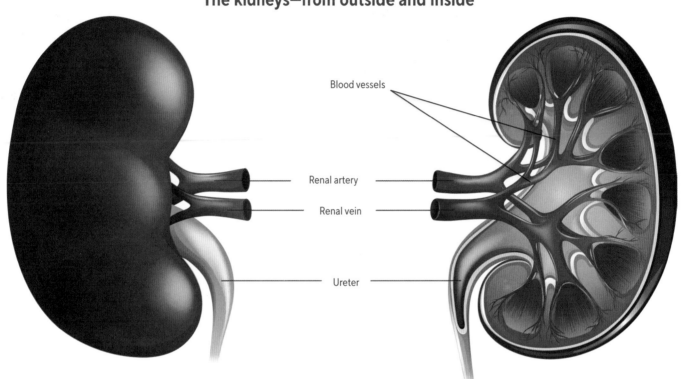

Blood vessels

Renal artery

Renal vein

Ureter

Rapid-FIRE ?

The liver and gall bladder

HOW HEAVY IS **OUR LIVER?**

An adult's liver weighs around 2.8 to 4 lbs—about as heavy as the brain.

Too much fluid can be harmful

IS DRINKING **TOO MUCH WATER BAD FOR THE BODY?**

Yes. The kidneys can't handle too much fluid too quickly and the salt in the blood gets diluted. Low salt can be dangerous.

WHAT WILL HAPPEN IF HALF OF **OUR LIVER IS CUT AWAY?**

It will regenerate within eight to 15 days.

HOW MANY FUNCTIONS DOES THE LIVER PERFORM?

About 500! Positioned at the upper right of our abdomen, the liver is the only organ that is also a gland. One of its functions is to store fat-soluble vitamins like A, E, and K. It also processes poisons in the blood and changes unwanted proteins into urea, which goes into urine.

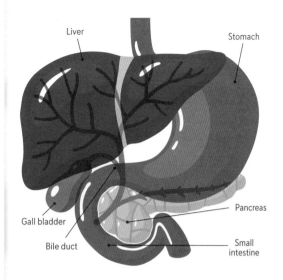

The bile duct and related organs

WHAT IS BILE?

Bile is a yellow-green liquid made by the liver and stored in the gall bladder. From there it passes into the small intestine where it helps break up fatty food. Bile is composed of acids, pigments, salts, water, and electrolyte chemicals. The human liver produces about 27 to 34 oz of bile every day.

WHERE IS URINE PRODUCED?

Urine is formed in the kidneys, which extract unwanted substances from the blood combining them with water to make urine that then passes through the ureters to the bladder.

HOW DOES THE KIDNEY FILTER BLOOD?

Inside our kidneys are filters called nephrons. Each nephron has two parts. The first part filters large molecules of toxins from the blood and other body fluids. The blood then passes through the next filter called the tubule. Here nutrients are added into our bloodstream and the remaining toxins filtered out.

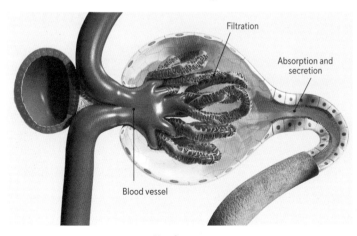

Nephron

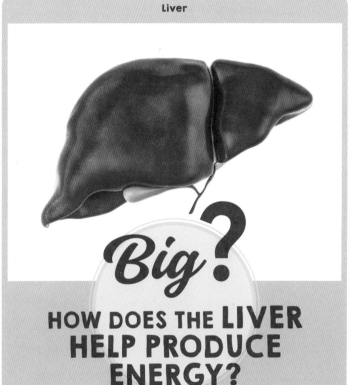

Liver

Big?

HOW DOES THE LIVER HELP PRODUCE ENERGY?

One of the liver's most important functions is processing digested food from the intestine and turning it into energy—a process called metabolism. For example, foods like potato and rice are broken down by the body and turned into a type of sugar called glucose, which is the main source of fuel for the body. The liver stores glucose as glycogen. When the body needs energy, the liver converts the glycogen back to glucose.

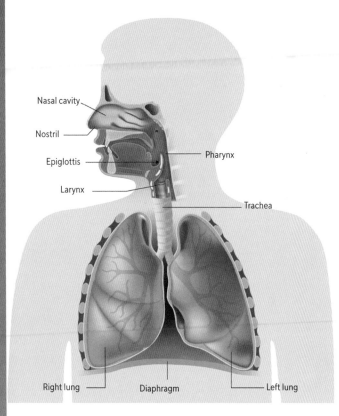

Nasal cavity

Nostril

Epiglottis

Pharynx

Larynx

Trachea

Right lung

Diaphragm

Left lung

The respiratory system

WHY DO WE BREATHE?

The human body can survive without food for a few days, and without water for less, but it cannot survive at all if breathing stops for more than a minute or two. Breathing provides every cell in the body with a continuous supply of oxygen. Without oxygen, the cells will quickly die.

WHY DO WE COUGH?

We cough when mucus, dust, or other particles clog the air passages between our nose and lungs. The sudden blast of air helps to clear the tubes.

Coughing

Rapid-FIRE ?

HOW MANY MILES OF AIRWAYS ARE THERE IN OUR LUNGS?

1,490 miles, which provide a huge area for oxygen to seep through into the blood in the short space of each breath.

HOW BIG IS A LUNG?

If laid out flat, a lung can cover an area the size of a tennis court.

Holding your breath

HOW MANY BREATHS DOES AN AVERAGE PERSON TAKE DURING A LIFETIME?

600 million breaths!

WHAT MAKES OUR BREATH FORM A CLOUD?

When we breathe out on a very cold day, water vapor in the air we breathe condenses into a mist of tiny water droplets.

Seeing your breath

WHAT IS A DIAPHRAGM?

The diaphragm is a domed sheet of muscle below the lungs that controls breathing. When we breathe in, the diaphragm flattens out, pulling the lungs down and expanding them so that they can draw in air. When we breathe out, the diaphragm expands to force air out of the lungs.

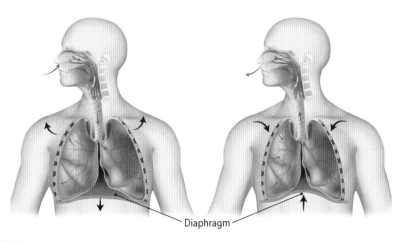

Diaphragm

Breathing in and out

WHY DOES RUNNING MAKE US PANT?

Muscles use up oxygen as they work. When we run, the muscles work hard and need extra oxygen. Panting makes us breathe in up to 20 times more air to supply our muscles with the oxygen that they need.

Runners in a road race

Inside the lungs

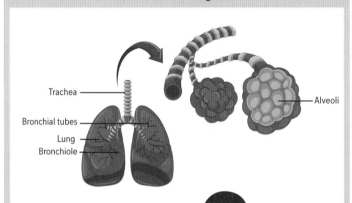

Trachea

Bronchial tubes

Lung

Bronchiole

Alveoli

Big ? WHAT HAPPENS WHEN WE BREATHE?

When we breathe in air through our nose or mouth, it flows down through the throat via a tube called the pharynx at the top, larynx in the middle, and trachea at the bottom. The trachea pipes air into the lungs, which are two spongy grayish-pink inflatable bags in our chest. Oxygen from the air passes into the bloodstream through tiny air sacs called alveoli in the lungs. The blood then carries the oxygen around the body. At the same time, unwanted carbon dioxide passes from the blood through the alveoli walls into the lungs and is finally expelled from the body as we breathe out.

WHAT ARE AEROBIC AND ANAEROBIC RESPIRATION?

Aerobic respiration is when muscle cells burn glucose (sugar) with oxygen to produce energy. Anaerobic respiration is when they burn glucose without oxygen. For example, during a sprint there is not enough time to boost the oxygen supply to the muscles, so anaerobic respiration takes place. Only on longer runs do they begin to work aerobically.

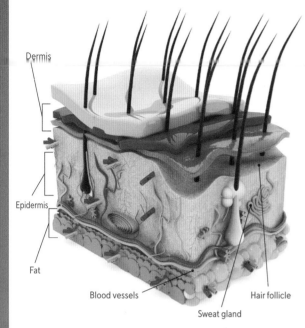

Dermis

Epidermis

Fat

Blood vessels

Hair follicle

Sweat gland

Layers and structure of the skin

DOES THE BODY NEED SKIN, HAIR, AND NAILS?

Skin, hair, and nails are part of the body's defenses. Skin is basically a protective barrier. Hair keeps us warm. Nails protect our fingers and toes as well as helping us grasp objects. Skin, hair, and nails contain keratin, a protein that makes them strong.

WHY DOES THE SKIN HAVE PORES?

The skin has tiny holes, called pores, to let out sweat. When we are too hot, glands under the skin pump out sweat or water, which cools us as it evaporates. These pores are all over the body and also secrete sebum, which is our natural body oil. Sebum helps the skin remain healthy.

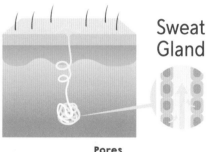

Sweat Gland

Pores

Rapid-FIRE?

Toenails

HOW FAST DOES A TOENAIL GROW?

Four times slower than a fingernail.

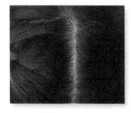

Thick hair

HOW MANY STRANDS OF HAIR DO WE HAVE?

On average, 100,000 to 150,000 strands.

Hair follicles

DOES HAIR GROW QUICKLY?

It is the second-fastest growing tissue in the body. The fastest is bone marrow.

WHAT IS SKIN MICROBIOTA?

It is the community of good bacteria on our skin.

WHAT GIVES HAIR AND SKIN THEIR COLOR?

A pigment called melanin. In the hair, melanin is in two forms: one lighter, causing blonde or red hair, the other darker, resulting in brown or black hair. The more melanin there is in the skin, the darker it is and the better protected it is from damaging sunlight.

Hair and skin color depends on melanin.

HOW MANY HAIRS FALL OUT EVERY DAY?

No hair lasts more than about six years. Every day we lose about 60 to 100 hairs, but since we have about 100,000 on our scalp, we hardly notice. After a while, new hairs grow from hair follicles. But the rate of fallout and regrowth is inherited from our family.

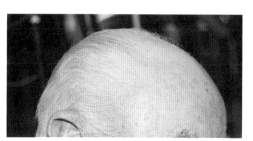

Hair loss is more common with age

WHY ARE NAILS PINK IN COLOR?

The nails on the ends of our fingers and toes are hard because they are made of a kind of protein called keratin. Little blood vessels known as capillaries allow blood to flow beneath the nails, which helps the nails to grow and gives them a pinkish color.

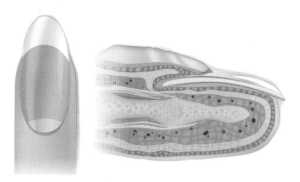

Fingernail

Big? HOW USEFUL IS OUR SKIN?

Sweat helps regulate body temperature

Very. It stops the moisture inside the body from drying out and prevents germs from getting in. A pigment called melanin in the skin shields us from the harmful rays of the Sun. The skin helps in regulating the body temperature, and its innermost layer stores water, fat, and other nutrients as well as producing hormones for the body. When part of the skin is wounded, it receives a greater supply of blood to deliver infection fighting substances that help it heal faster.

WHAT IS THE EXCRETORY SYSTEM?

It is the system in the body that is responsible for the excretion (removal) of broken-down waste from our food in solid and liquid forms. The urinary and renal organs, including the kidneys, ureters, bladder, and urethra, are the main excretory organs. The intestines are also involved. The lungs and the liver play a role too.

The urinary system

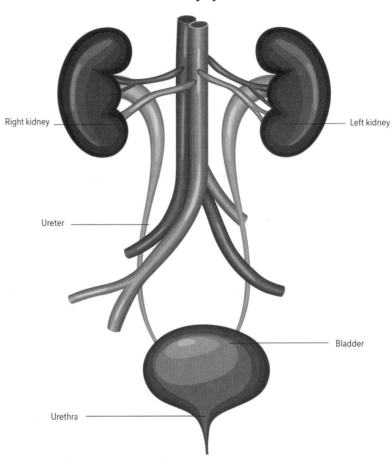

Right kidney

Left kidney

Ureter

Bladder

Urethra

WHAT DOES HUMAN SOLID WASTE CONSIST OF?

The solid waste in our large intestine leaves the body via the anus, and is called poop or feces. Though solid, it actually consists of 75 percent water. Out of the remaining 25 percent, one-third is dead bacteria, and one-third is undigested food. The rest of it contains fats, cholesterol, compounds of calcium and iron, small amounts of protein, cell waste, and bile. A healthy adult usually discharges solid waste no more than twice daily. If they need to go to the bathroom much more or less often, it may cause discomfort such as stomachache.

The intestines

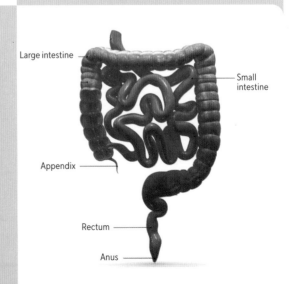

Large intestine

Small intestine

Appendix

Rectum

Anus

DO THE LUNGS ALSO HELP US GET RID OF UNWANTED SUBSTANCES?

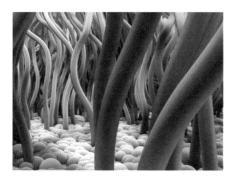

Cilia in the lungs

Though the lungs are not the most important part of excretion, they do play a role. Our lungs have tiny fibers known as cilia, and when we breathe in any unwanted particles, they get trapped in the mucus present in the cilia. Those particles come out when we cough.

HOW IS URINE CARRIED FROM THE KIDNEYS TO THE URINARY BLADDER?

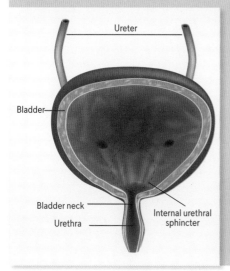

Ureter

Bladder

Bladder neck

Urethra

Internal urethral sphincter

The bladder and the ureters

Urine, or pee, is waste disposed of by our bodies in the form of liquid. The ureters are tubelike structures which start from the abdomen area. Each ureter arises from a funnel-like structure inside one kidney. The main function of the ureters is to carry urine from the kidneys to the urinary bladder.

Rapid-FIRE ?

WHAT ARE TWO COMMON DISORDERS OF THE EXCRETORY SYSTEM?

Diarrhea and constipation.

Excreting solid waste

WHAT ARE SPHINCTERS?

Internal urethral sphincter

sphincter

Circular muscles that prevent urine or feces coming out by accident.

WHEN DO WE FEEL LIKE PEEING?

When our bladder is half full, it gives us the signal to "go."

HOW ARE TOXINS REMOVED FROM THE BODY?

We gather toxins throughout the day. Once the body identifies them, the liver dumps them into the bile, which then transports the toxins to the small intestine. The toxins are then flushed out of the intestinal tract.

WHAT IS THE FUNCTION OF THE URETHRA?

It transports urine from the bladder out of the body. The urethra is nearly 7.8 inches long in males. In females it is much shorter, at around 1.5 inches.

WHAT IS THE NERVOUS SYSTEM?

The network of tissues that transmits signals between the different parts of the body is called the nervous system. It triggers and coordinates the body's actions in response to its environment. This network has two parts: the central nervous system, or CNS, and the peripheral nervous system, or PNS. The CNS mainly consists of the brain and spinal cord, while the PNS is made up of nerves connecting the CNS to the body's organs and tissues.

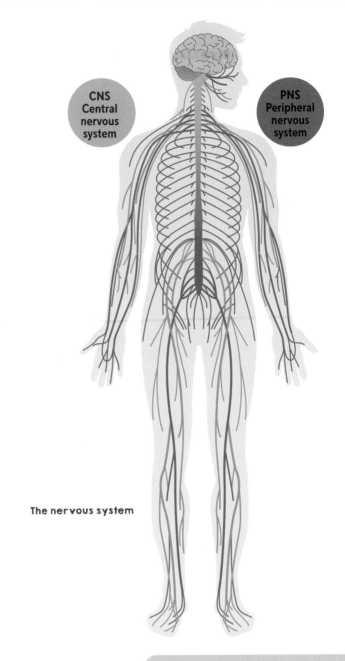

CNS
Central nervous system

PNS
Peripheral nervous system

The nervous system

Big? WHAT ARE NERVES?

Nerves are fibers that carry messages through the body. They are made of cells called neurons and are coated in a fatty substance called myelin that protects the nerves as well as helping the messages travel fast to their destination. Sound, light, smell, taste, and touch are detected by nerves and this information is relayed to the CNS. The CNS processes the information and sends a signal to a particular body part to activate it.

Structure of a Neuron

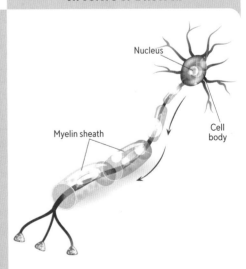

Nucleus

Myelin sheath

Cell body

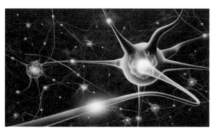

IS THERE **ELECTRICITY IN THE BODY?**

Yes. The nervous system can be compared to the electrical wiring in your home. At the end of each neuron in our nerves is a synaptic terminal which releases chemicals called neurotransmitters that move the electrical signal forward to the next neuron. When a muscle has to be "switched on," electrical impulses travel along the nerves to that muscle or part of the body carrying messages to make them work as needed.

How neurons pass signals

HOW MANY **NEURONS ARE THERE IN YOUR BODY?**

About one billion!

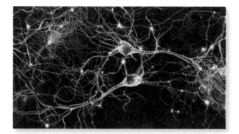

Network of neurons

WHAT IS THE **SPINAL CORD?**

The body's largest nerve. The spinal cord runs through the center of the spine.

The spinal cord

HOW **FAST DO NERVE SIGNALS TRAVEL?**

The fastest travel at 393 ft per second.

WHAT ARE THE **SOMATIC AND AUTONOMOUS NERVOUS SYSTEMS?**

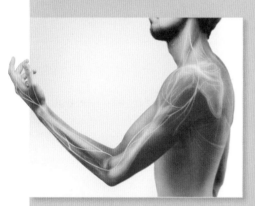

Nerves in the arm

They are parts of the PNS. We control the somatic system, and its job is to carry signals to the skeletal muscles for them to perform physical activities like walking, lifting, typing, etc. On the other hand, the autonomous system works automatically to perform functions like making our heart beat and the glands secrete juices.

HOW DO **REFLEXES WORK?**

When we touch something very hot or get pricked by a needle, we snatch our hand back very quickly, without thinking. This is called a reflex action. It is an emergency response of the nervous system where the information does not first go to the brain but is acted upon immediately at the place of discomfort.

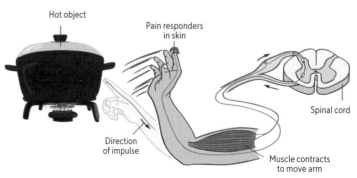

Hot object

Pain responders in skin

Spinal cord

Direction of impulse

Muscle contracts to move arm

Reflex action

WHAT IS REPRODUCTION?

Having babies is known as reproduction. A man's reproductive organs make millions of tiny cells called sperm, which are like tiny tadpoles. A woman's reproductive organs release an egg into her uterus, or womb, at a certain time every month. One of the man's sperm works its way into an egg and fertilizes it. The fertilized egg grows gradually inside the woman's uterus, until, after nine months, a baby is born.

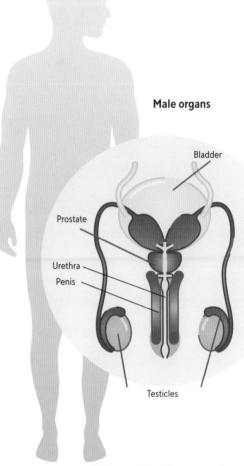

Male organs

Bladder

Prostate

Urethra

Penis

Testicles

The reproductive organs

WHAT IS MENSTRUATION?

Menstruation is the monthly cycle of changes in a woman's body that prepares her for having a baby. Every four weeks, one of her ovaries releases an egg that slides down the fallopian tube and into her uterus. If the egg is not then fertilized, the lining of the uterus breaks down and the blood and tissue is discarded by the body from the vagina.

Big?

WHAT IS PUBERTY?

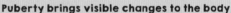
Puberty brings visible changes to the body

We are born with reproductive, or sexual, organs, but they only develop enough for us to have children once we reach the age of puberty—typically 11–13 years old. At puberty, chemicals called sex hormones flood the body, stimulating the changes that turn boys into men and girls into women. When a boy reaches puberty, his testicles grow and begin to produce sperm. When a girl reaches puberty, she begins to grow breasts and her monthly periods, or menstruation, start.

WHAT ARE TESTICLES?

The two testicles are the other main male reproductive organs. They have two functions: one is to produce sperm and the other is to make a hormone called testosterone. The testicles are vulnerable since they hang outside the body, so they are made up of strong, fibrous tissue called tunica.

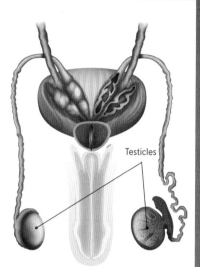

The testicles

Female organs

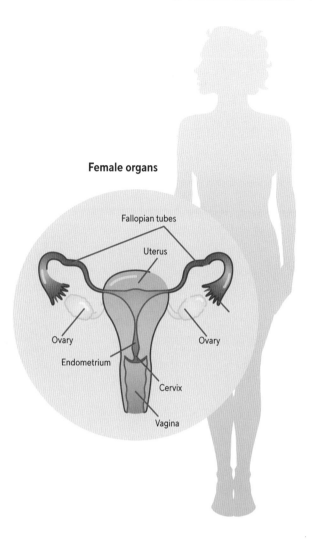

Fallopian tubes

Uterus

Ovary

Ovary

Endometrium

Cervix

Vagina

WHAT ARE THE PENIS AND THE VAGINA?

The penis is one of the two main male reproductive organs. Positioned just above the testicles, it is a bundle of spongy tissue. The vagina is a tubular, muscular, elastic canal in the female body that leads to the uterus. The male penis becomes erect when filled with blood and is inserted in the vagina where it releases sperm.

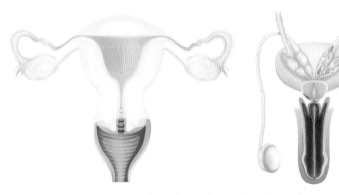

The female vagina and male penis

Rapid-FIRE ?

WHERE ARE THE LARGEST AND SMALLEST HUMAN CELLS PRODUCED?

In the reproductive organs. The sperm is the smallest and the egg is the largest.

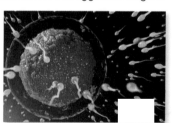

Sperm and egg

WHAT HAPPENS TO SPERM THAT ARE NOT RELEASED?

They are absorbed back into the blood.

IS THE APPEARANCE OF BODY HAIR IN BOYS AND GIRLS A SIGN OF PUBERTY?

Yes.

WHAT IS PREGNANCY?

When a baby is developing inside a woman's uterus, this is known as pregnancy. The developing baby is known as an embryo when it is very tiny, and then as a fetus until it is born. The whole process from the fertilization of the egg to a fully grown baby usually takes about 270 days, or 38 weeks. Pregnancy goes through three stages called trimesters: the first is from week one to week 12; the second from week 13 to week 28; and the weeks after that are the third trimester.

| Fertilized egg | 2-cell stage | 4-cell stage | 8-cell stage | 16-cell stage | Blastocyst |

   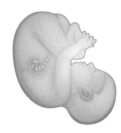

Fetus - 4 weeks   Fetus - 10 weeks

Fetus - 16 weeks   Fetus - 20 weeks

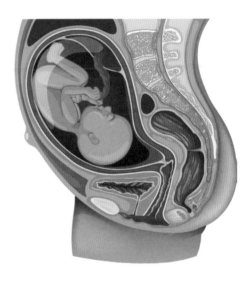

The development of a baby in the mother's uterus

Rapid-FIRE ?

HOW MANY DAYS DOES IT TAKE FOR THE BRAIN, HEART, AND EYES TO FORM?

Around 35 days.

HOW MANY EGGS DOES A FEMALE PRODUCE DURING HER LIFETIME?

None. She is born with them.

HOW MUCH DOES A NEWBORN WEIGH?

The average newborn baby weighs about 7.7 lbs.

A newborn baby

HOW FAST DOES AN UNBORN BABY GROW?

A human grows faster inside the uterus than at any other time. Three weeks after the egg is fertilized, the embryo is the size of a grain of rice. Five weeks later, almost every part of the baby has formed—yet it is only the size of a thumb. By the time it is born, the baby will probably be about 19 inches long.

Checking a baby's development with an ultrasound scan

HOW DOES AN UNBORN BABY EAT?

When the egg is fertilized and the embryo forms, a temporary organ known as the placenta forms alongside. Food and oxygen from the mother's blood are carried by the umbilical cord through the placenta into the blood of the growing baby. It is important for the mother to eat well so that the baby receives the right nutrition.

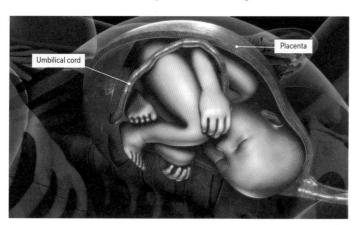

Umbilical cord

Placenta

A baby in the uterus

WHERE DO THE SPERM AND THE EGG COME FROM?

Sperm are made in the testicles. After puberty, the testicles make millions of sperm every day. When a girl is born, she already has up to two million eggs stored in her two ovaries. After puberty, one of these eggs is released every month to travel down to the uterus.

HOW ARE TWINS FORMED?

Sometimes a fertilized egg can split into two. When this happens a pair of babies are formed, and because they have developed from one egg, they are identical. It could also happen that two eggs are fertilized at the same time and two babies develop in the uterus. While these babies are also twins, they are not identical.

Big?

WHAT ARE THE FIRST SIGNS OF PREGNANCY?

Listening to the baby's heartbeat

The first hints are a missed menstruation cycle, feeling sick in the mornings, and heaviness in the breasts. A simple test can check whether a woman is pregnant or not. By the 16th, or at the latest 20th week, the heartbeat of the fetus can be heard through a stethoscope.

HOW ARE HUMANS AND ANIMALS DIFFERENT?

Humans belong to group of animals called Chordata. All chordates have a bilaterally symmetrical body, which means that the right side and the left side are mirror images of each other on the exterior. They also have backbones. But humans differ significantly from animals in two major ways: they stand upright, on two legs, and they have larger, highly developed brains.

Brain size comparison between a human, a fish, and a bird

Big? WHAT IS AN ORGAN SYSTEM?

The human body is made up of trillions of tiny cells. A group of cells performing the same function is called tissue, and tissues make up an organ. An organ performs a specific function in the body, and a group of organs make up a system that performs an operation fundamental to the body. For example, the digestive system handles the food we eat and its absorption, and the lymphatic system keeps us protected from germs. There are 11 organ systems in the body: the cardiovascular, digestive, endocrine, lymphatic, nervous, muscular, reproductive, skeletal, respiratory, urinary, and skin systems.

The organs of the digestive system

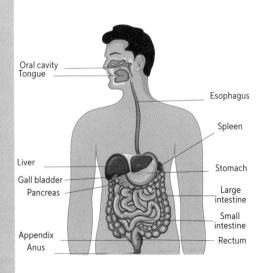

Oral cavity
Tongue
Esophagus
Spleen
Liver
Stomach
Gall bladder
Pancreas
Large intestine
Small intestine
Appendix
Anus
Rectum

HOW MANY ORGANS DOES THE BODY HAVE?

It is often said that there are 78 organs in the human body, but scientists do not agree on this number, and some say that there are up to 100. What everyone agrees on is that there are five vital organs, that need to be functioning well for the body to survive. These are the brain, heart, kidney, liver, and lungs. They differ in size, shape, location, and function, and belong to different organ systems.

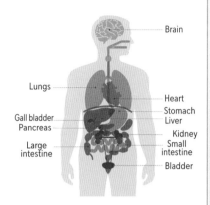

Some organs in the human body

WHAT IS METABOLISM?

The human body needs energy to function, and energy comes from food. The process through which food is converted into energy is called metabolism.

WHAT IS AGING?

As a newborn child grows, its body becomes bigger, stronger, and smarter for many years, until it reaches adulthood. After some time, as the years pass, the body's organs start becoming weaker and less efficient. The brain, which also grows as the child grows, starts shrinking, especially after the age of 75. The decline of the body over the years is called aging.

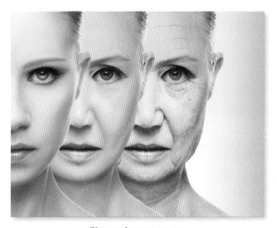

The aging process

Rapid-FIRE?

ARE THERE BACTERIA IN THE HUMAN BODY?

Yes, there are equal numbers of human cells and bacteria in the body.

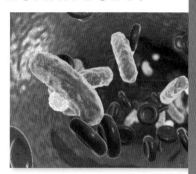

Bacteria and blood cells

HOW MANY BREATHS DO WE TAKE EACH DAY?

Between 17,000 and 26,000.

Breathing

HOW MUCH WATER IS THERE IN OUR BODIES?

About 65 percent of the human body is made of water.

Water in the body

DO CELLS DIE EVERY DAY?

Yes, many tens of thousands of old cells die, and new cells form, every second!

WHAT IS A SKELETON?

The skeleton is the strong but remarkably mobile framework of the body. It has two main parts. The axial skeleton consists of the skull, spine, ribs, and sternum (breastbone). The appendicular skeleton consists of the arms and legs, shoulders, and pelvis (hip bone)—basically, those bones that are attached to or hang from the axial skeleton.

Rapid-FIRE ?

HOW MANY BONES DO THE HAND AND FOOT HAVE?

The hand has 27 bones, while the foot has 26.

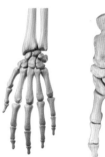
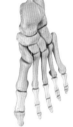

Bones of the hand and foot

DO ALL HUMANS HAVE THE SAME NUMBER OF RIBS?

Most humans have 12 ribs, but a few have 13.

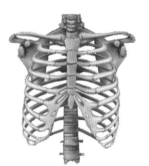

Rib cage

HOW STRONG ARE OUR BONES?

They are stronger than steel of the same size and shape!

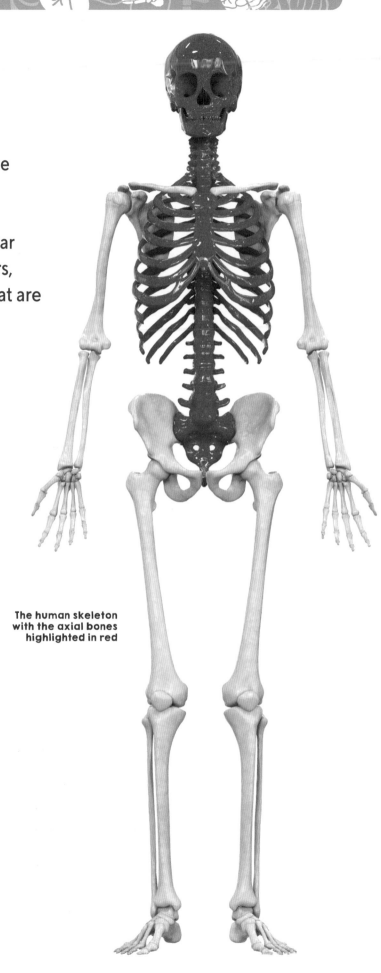

The human skeleton with the axial bones highlighted in red

IS THE **HEAD MADE OF A SINGLE BONE?**

No, it is made up of 22 separate bones that fit tightly together like a jigsaw puzzle. The lower jaw is the only bone with a moveable joint. The head is not connected to the neck but rests on the uppermost bone of the spine. This allows it to nod or move up and down.

WHAT IS THE DIFFERENCE BETWEEN **MALE AND FEMALE SKELETONS?**

The difference is the pelvic bone. Females have a more rounded pelvis than males. But there are other subtle differences too. In general, male skeletons are larger and heavier since the bones are longer and thicker. The skeleton of a female is fully formed by the age of 18, while the skeleton of a male is fully developed by 21 years old.

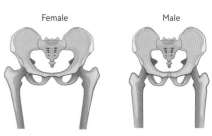

Female   Male

The pelvic bones

WHERE CAN WE FIND **BONE MARROW?**

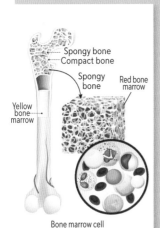

Spongy bone
Compact bone
Spongy bone
Red bone marrow
Yellow bone marrow
Bone marrow cell

Bone marrow

In the hollow center of the breastbone, ribs, and hips is the soft, spongy, red bone marrow where red and white blood cells are created. All our bones have this red marrow when we are born but, as we grow older, the marrow of long bones such as the legs and arms turns yellow.

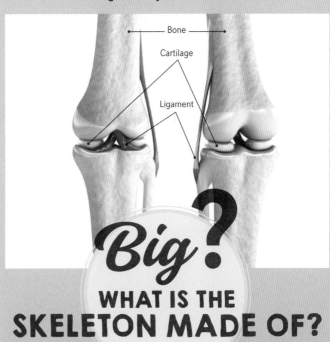

Cartilage at the joint between bones

Bone
Cartilage
Ligament

Big? WHAT IS THE **SKELETON MADE OF?**

The body has many bones, which, when put together as a framework, make up the skeletal system. There are over 200 bones, and they are linked by a rubbery substance called cartilage. Bones are very tough and light because their outside is made from a mixture of hard minerals such as calcium, and stringy, elastic collagen. Inside the tough, dry casing, there are holes called lacunae, full of living cells known as osteocytes, which are bathed in blood—just like every other cell in the body.

WHICH IS THE **LONGEST BONE IN THE BODY?**

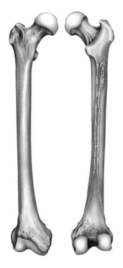

It is the thigh bone, or femur, and it makes up over a quarter of an adult's height. The head of this bone has a ball-and-socket joint which fits into the hip, enabling the leg to move. A well-developed adult femur can bear a load of up to 2,400 pounds.

Thigh bones

WHAT IS A JOINT?

Joints allow the bones of the skeleton to move. The shoulders and hips are ball-and-socket joints. The knees and elbows are hinges (like the hinges that let a door open and close). The neck joint allows the head to rotate. The joints between the backbones are connected by layers of cartilage that are stiff but allow a little movement. Knee joints are helped to move slowly by capsules of oil called synovial fluid, and so are called synovial joints.

Ball-and-socket shoulder joint

Rapid-FIRE ?

IS THE **KNEE BONE AN ACTUAL BONE IN INFANTS?**

No. It is cartilage for the first few years.

Baby's knees

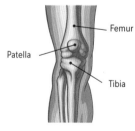

Femur
Patella
Tibia

Knee joints

WHICH IS THE **BIGGEST JOINT IN THE BODY?**

The knee joint. It connects three bones: the femur, tibia, and patella.

WHAT BONE IS THE **ONLY ONE NOT CONNECTED TO ANOTHER?**

The hyoid bone in our throat.

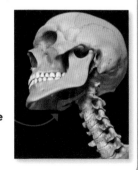

Hyoid bone

WHAT IS THE **STRUCTURE OF A BONE?**

Bone is made up of living tissue divided into three types. The outer tissue is strong and compact. Inside that is the spongy meshlike tissue, which is where blood vessels carry nutrients for the bone. At each end of the bone is smooth subchondral tissue where cartilage forms.

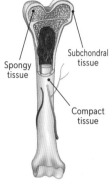

Spongy tissue
Subchondral tissue
Compact tissue

Bone structure

WHY **DON'T JOINTS SQUEAK?**

Joints are cushioned by soft, squashy cartilage. The cavities of several joints contain synovial fluid, which works like oil to keep them moving smoothly. Eating Omega-3 fatty acids, found in fish, brussels sprouts, and flax seeds among other foods, helps us keep a healthy amount of synovial fluid in our joints.

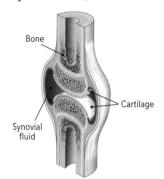

Bone
Cartilage
Synovial fluid

Bone, cartilage, synovial fluid

WHAT ARE **LIGAMENTS?**

They are strong, flexible straps of tissue which connect a bone to the one next to it. Ligaments are basically a kind of fiber. The main role of a ligament is to hold our bones properly so that the skeleton stays stable and the joints do not move out of place.

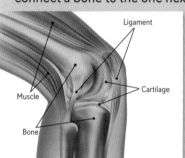

Ligament
Muscle
Cartilage
Bone

Bone, cartilage, ligament, muscle

Big **?**
WHAT ARE THE **VARIOUS TYPES OF BONES?**

Long bones
Short bones

Bones of the arm and hand

Bones are categorized by their shapes. Long bones are longer than they are wide. They are the most mobile parts of the skeleton, such as the arm bones. Short bones are almost similar in length and thickness, such as the wrist and ankles. Flat bones are curved, thin bones that provide protection to organs. Sesamoid bones are small, and are found in places like the wrist and feet. They provide protection against high force or pressure. Irregular bones don't have any particular shape. They are found in the face and the spine.

CAN **BONES FUSE TOGETHER?**

When we are born, we have nearly 300 separate bones. As we grow up, some of these bones merge together. This process continues until we are about 25 years old. By the time our skeleton stops growing, we have 206 bones in the body.

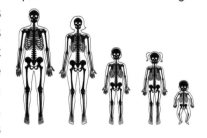

The skeleton as it grows

WHY DO WE NEED MUSCLES?

Every move we make—running, dancing, smiling, and everything else—depends on muscles. We even need muscles to sit still: without them, we would slump like a rag doll. In the muscles we use for movement, there are thousands of long fibers, each made up of hundreds of thinner strands called myofibrils.

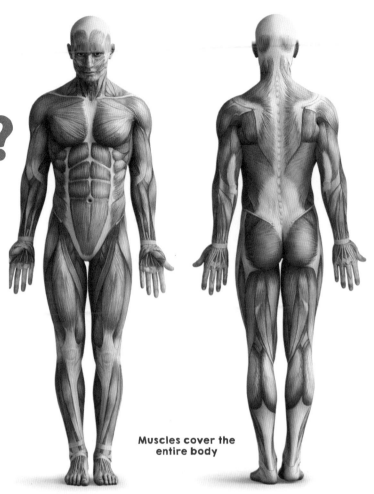

Muscles cover the entire body

DO MUSCLES PRODUCE HEAT?

Muscles build up almost 85 percent of our total body heat. When we are very cold and are shivering, it is the rapid contraction and relaxation of muscles that produces heat.

Big?
WHAT ARE THE TWO DIFFERENT KINDS OF MUSCLES?

Muscles are bundles of fibers that tense and relax to move different parts of the body. There are two kinds: muscles that we can control, called voluntary muscles, and muscles that we can't, called involuntary muscles. Most voluntary muscles are skeletal muscles: these move parts of the body when we want them to. Involuntary muscles are those like our heart and those around our digestive system, which work automatically, without us thinking about it.

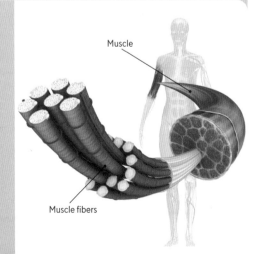

Bundles of muscle fibers

Muscle

Muscle fibers

ARE ALL **MUSCLES STRIPY?**

Alternate bands of different filaments give muscles a stripy look. But not all muscles are stripy. Smooth muscles contract blood vessels to control blood flow to the gut to push food through. The heart is powered by the smooth "cardiac" muscle, which beats automatically, though its rate may vary.

HOW MANY MUSCLES ### ARE THERE?

The body is covered with an almost complete envelope of skeletal muscle pairs, which make up 40 percent of the body's weight. There are more than 600, the largest of which is the gluteus maximus in the buttock. Most work in pairs.

Working out the muscles

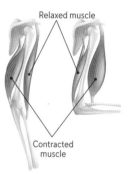

Rapid-FIRE ?

WHY DO MUSCLES COME IN PAIRS?

One of the pair contracts to bend a joint while the other relaxes, and when the joint has to be straightened again, the roles switch.

Relaxed muscle

Contracted muscle

Lifting your forearm

WHY DO MUSCLES NEED AN OXYGEN BOOST?

When the muscles work hard, they need more oxygen to burn sugar.

You need to breathe faster when you run.

WHERE IS THE **SMALLEST MUSCLE?**

In the inner ear.

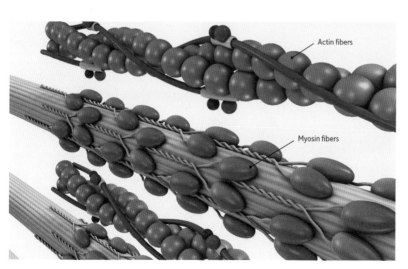

Actin fibers

Myosin fibers

HOW DO **MUSCLES CONTRACT?**

In the muscle fibers, filaments of actin and myosin interlock. When the brain sends the muscle a message to contract (or tense), little buds on each myosin filament twist sharply, pulling on actin filaments and contracting.

Muscle fibers

WHY ARE THE SENSES IMPORTANT?

Our senses tell us what is going on around us. We have five main senses: sight from our eyes, hearing from our ears, smell from our nose, taste from our tongue, and touch from most of our skin. Senses pick up sensations, some from inside the body, some from outside, and feed them to the brain via the nerves.

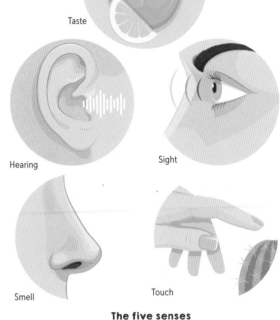

Taste

Hearing

Sight

Smell

Touch

The five senses

Enjoying being tickled

WHAT ARE TOUCH RECEPTORS?

There are touch receptors all over the body, embedded in the skin. They react to four kinds of feelings—a light touch, steady pressure, heat and cold, and pain.

Big?

HOW DO THE EYES WORK?

The eyes are two tough little balls filled with a jellylike substance called vitreous humor. Eyes are a bit like video cameras. A lens at the front projects the picture onto the back of the eye, called the retina, where millions of light-sensitive cells detect the picture and transmit it to the brain via the optic nerve. Each eye gives a slightly different view of the world. The brain combines these different views to give a complete 3D picture.

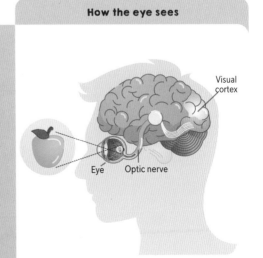

How the eye sees

Visual cortex

Eye

Optic nerve

WHAT IS THE FUNCTION OF THE OUTER EAR?

The flap of skin on the outside of our head is only one part of the ear, called the outer ear. It funnels sound down a passage called the ear canal into our head. The real workings of the ear are inside our head. There the bones of the middle ear and the curly tube of the inner ear process the sound.

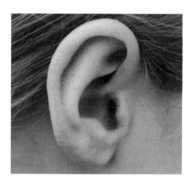

The outer ear

Rapid-FIRE ?

WHAT IS THE IRIS?

It is a circular membrane in the eye that controls the amount of light that goes through the pupil to the retina.

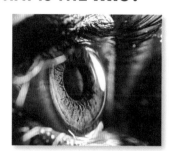

The iris surrounds the dark pupil

HOW DOES THE EAR DETECT A SOUND'S DIRECTION?

By the tiny differences in volume—the ear closer to the source will hear the sound louder.

Listening to sound

WHAT IS THE BACK OF THE TONGUE SENSITIVE TO?

The bitter taste.

HOW DO WE SMELL?

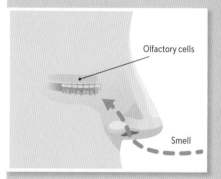

Olfactory cells

Smell

How the sense of smell works

Specialized sensory receptors called olfactory cells help us smell. Found deep inside our nose on a small patch of nerves, these cells react to minute traces of chemicals in the air. Once these traces are detected, a message is sent to our brain, which identifies the smell.

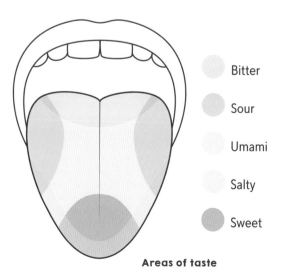

Bitter

Sour

Umami

Salty

Sweet

Areas of taste

HOW MANY TASTE RECEPTORS DOES THE TONGUE HAVE?

As stated before, the tongue has five different kinds of taste receptors, called taste buds. They react to sweet, salty, bitter, sour, and umami tastes in food. Although all parts of the tongue can detect these five tastes, different parts are more sensitive to a specific one.

HOW DO WE SEE?

We see an object when light bounces off it and enters our eyes. The black circle in the middle of the eye is called the pupil. Light passes through the pupil and is focused by the lens onto the retina at the back of the eye. The retina sends signals to the brain, and the brain then composes the image for visual identification.

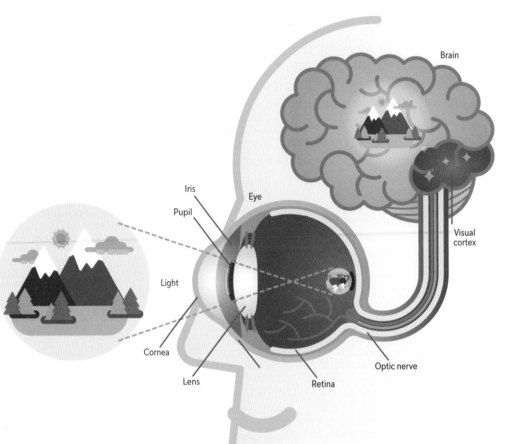

Brain

Iris

Eye

Pupil

Visual cortex

Light

Cornea

Optic nerve

Lens

Retina

The way we see

Big?

WHY DO PEOPLE HAVE EYES OF DIFFERENT COLORS?

The iris is the colored ring around the pupil. Its color comes from a substance called melanin. Brown irises have a lot of melanin, while blue ones lack it. Variations in melanin result in pigments like green and shades of brown or gray. In some people, different color shades are found in the same eye. This is because different parts of the iris produce differing amounts of melanin.

Eyes of different colors

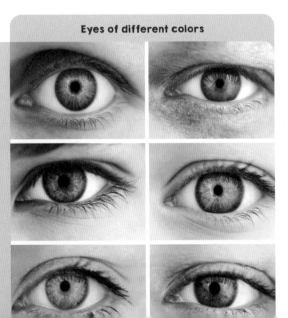

WHY DO WE HAVE
TWO EYES?

Two eyes help us to judge how far away something is. Each eye sees a slightly different picture, which the brain combines into a single, three-dimensional, or 3D, picture—one that has depth as well as height and breadth.

WHY DO **WE BLINK?**

We blink to clean our eyes. Each eye is covered with a thin film of salty fluid, so every time we blink, the eyelid washes the eyeball and wipes away dust and germs. The water drains away through a narrow tube into the nose.

The tear duct is at the inner corner of the eye.

HOW DO
WE SEE COLOR?

Nerve cells in the retina, called cones, react to the colors red, blue, and green. These combine to make up all the colors. The cones only work well in bright light, which is why we can't see color when it gets dark. It is said that the human eye can see 10 million colors!

WHY DOES THE
PUPIL CHANGE SIZE?

The iris, a circular muscle, controls the size of the pupil. The pupil becomes smaller in bright light to stop too much light from damaging the retina. In low light the pupil opens to let in more light.

Rapid-FIRE?

WHAT ARE **FLOATERS?**

Protein strands floating inside the eye, creating shadows on the retina.

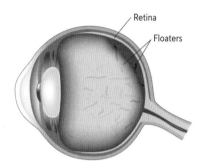

Retina

Floaters

Floaters in the eye

WHAT IS THE CORNEA?

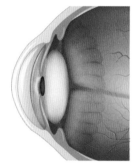

The transparent outer covering of the iris and the pupil.

Detail showing the cornea

HOW BIG IS THE **EYEBALL?**

An adult eyeball is about the size of a golf ball, but most of it is hidden inside the head.

DO OUR **EYES GROW?**

No. They remain the same size throughout our lives.

In the dark

In bright light

Different pupil sizes

WHY DO WE EAT?

The food we eat

The food we eat is used as fuel by our bodies. It is converted into energy that is needed to keep our various body functions going. Substances like carbohydrates and fats in food provide the most energy. Protein in our food helps us repair and build basic body cells. Natural chemicals called vitamins and minerals are necessary for the body to perform vital functions to keep it healthy.

HOW LONG ARE THE INTESTINES?

An adult's small intestine is 20 ft long—more than three times as long as the whole body! The length of the large intestine is five feet.

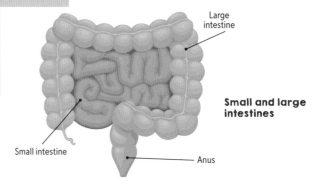

Small and large intestines

Large intestine

Small intestine

Anus

Big? WHERE DOES FOOD GO WHEN WE EAT IT?

Food moves through the digestive system, also called the alimentary canal or gut, as it is gradually broken down and absorbed. First it is chewed and softened in the mouth, and then it goes down the esophagus or food pipe into the stomach. There it is churned and mixed with strong acids and powerful enzymes, which break it down. After this, it goes into the tube called the small intestine where the nourishing part is absorbed into the blood, digest into the large intestine, where the waste is made solid. This is pushed out by the body in the form of feces, or poop, when we use the toilet.

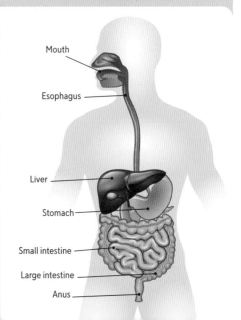

The alimentary canal

Mouth

Esophagus

Liver

Stomach

Small intestine

Large intestine

Anus

HOW DO WE TASTE FOODS?

Taste is one of the five senses. When we chew food, tiny particles of it dissolve in the watery saliva inside the mouth. The food stimulates the taste receptor cells, which are located on thousands of taste buds in the mouth—mostly on the tongue. Buds on different parts of the tongue react to different tastes.

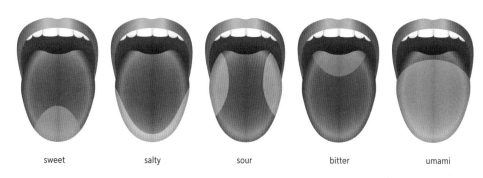

sweet   salty   sour   bitter   umami

The taste buds

WHY DOES VOMIT TASTE SOUR?

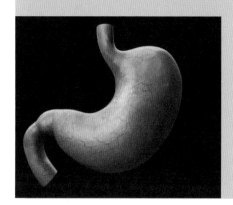

Once the food enters the stomach, it mixes with acid produced by the stomach to help digest it. When we vomit, we bring back this partially digested food into the mouth, and it tastes sour because of the acid in it.

The stomach

WHAT IS THE EPIGLOTTIS?

The trapdoor-like flap that closes off our windpipes when we swallow food. It stops food from going into the lungs, making sure that it goes down to the stomach, where it is meant to go.

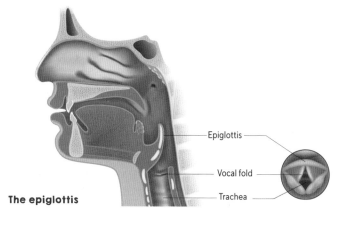

Epiglottis

Vocal fold

Trachea

The epiglottis

Rapid-FIRE ?

WHY ARE TEETH DIFFERENT SHAPES?

So that they can perform different functions: chewing, slicing, and grinding various types of food.

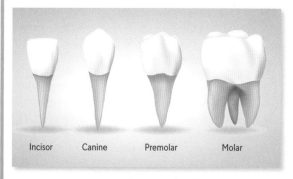

Incisor   Canine   Premolar   Molar

Types of human teeth

HOW LONG DOES FOOD REMAIN IN THE ALIMENTARY CANAL?

About 24 hours, from the time of swallowing to being pushed out as waste.

WHAT IS PERISTALSIS?

The process by which food advances through the gut, moved by ripples of muscles in the gut wall.

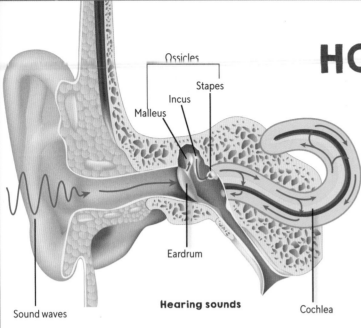

Ossicles

Stapes

Incus

Malleus

Eardrum

Sound waves

Hearing sounds

Cochlea

HOW DO WE **HEAR SOUND?**

Sound reaches our ears as a vibration in the air. The vibration travels through the outer ear to the eardrum, which makes the tiny bones in the middle ear vibrate, too. These pass the vibrations to the fluid around the cochlea in the inner ear. Nerve endings in the cochlea then send the signal to our brain to process.

HOW IS **SOUND MEASURED?**

The loudness of a sound is measured in decibels. The sound of a pin dropping is less than 10 decibels, while headphones make about 80 decibels. A noise over 120 decibels can damage our hearing.

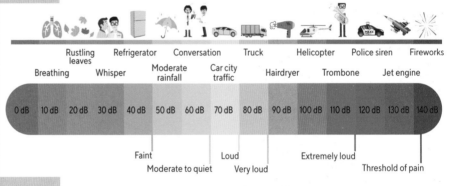

	Rustling leaves	Refrigerator		Conversation		Truck		Helicopter		Police siren		Fireworks		
Breathing		Whisper	Moderate rainfall		Car city traffic		Hairdryer		Trombone		Jet engine			
0 dB	10 dB	20 dB	30 dB	40 dB	50 dB	60 dB	70 dB	80 dB	90 dB	100 dB	110 dB	120 dB	130 dB	140 dB

Faint

Moderate to quiet

Loud

Very loud

Extremely loud

Threshold of pain

Measuring decibels

*Rapid-*FIRE **?**

WHAT ARE THE **SMALLEST BONES IN THE HUMAN BODY?**

The ossicles in the middle ear.

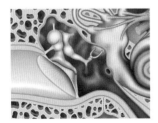

The ossicles

DO OUR **EARS "SLEEP"?**

No. They are always working, but our brain responds less to sound when we are asleep.

The ears don't sleep.

ARE THE **TWO EARS EQUALLY RESPONSIVE TO DIFFERENT KINDS OF SOUND?**

The right ear is more responsive to speech, while the left ear is more responsive to music.

Difference in sensitivity

DOES EARWAX HAVE ANY USEFUL FUNCTION?

Earwax is produced in our outer ear by skin glands. It is a yellow-brown substance found throughout the skin lining of the ear canal. The role of this wax is to prevent dust and other small particles from entering the ear. It also traps harmful microbes which can infect us.

HOW DO EARS HELP US BALANCE?

Three tubes in the inner ear, called the semicircular canals, are filled with fluid and fine hair. As we move, the fluid moves, and the hairs detect the motion of our head. Nerves in the lining of the tubes take this information and send it to the brain, which decides whether we are balanced or not.

Semicircular canals

Keeping our balance

WHY DO OUR EARS POP?

If we are flying in an airplane and it changes height quickly, our hearing may become muffled, because the air inside and outside the eardrum is at different pressures. Our ears "pop" when the pressures become equal again.

Changing pressure on the ears

Big?
WHAT IS THE ROLE OF MIDDLE AND INNER EARS?

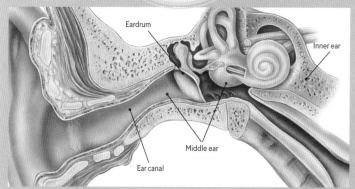
Eardrum

Inner ear

Middle ear

Ear canal

Inside the ear

The middle ear is the sound amplifier. Sound entering the middle ear hits a taut wall of skin called the eardrum, shaking it rapidly. As it shakes, it rattles three tiny bones, or ossicles, called the malleus (hammer), the incus (anvil), and the stapes (stirrup). These vibrations are then carried to the inner ear, which is mainly a curly tube full of fluid, called the cochlea. The rattling ossicles create waves in the fluid. Minute detector hairs waggle in these waves and, as they move, they send signals along the nerves to the brain.

CAN WE TALK WITHOUT WORDS?

Yes, people who are unable to hear or speak can use sign language. Sign language is highly developed, with its own grammar, and is used across the world, though there is no single language. Gestures are made using fingers, hands, and facial expressions to indicate a specific message.

Communicating
without speaking

Big? WHAT ARE THE VARIOUS WAYS OF COMMUNICATING?

American Sign Language alphabet

There are four main modes of communication: Verbal, nonverbal, written, and visual. Verbal is when we converse through speech or use sign language. Nonverbal is through body language, gestures, and facial expressions, and recognizable symbols such as traffic signals and street signs. Written communication is through writing, texting, emails, and via books and other printed material. Visual communication is through photographs, art, visual mediums such as television and film, and internet-based programs.

WHY IS VIDEOCONFERENCING POPULAR?

It is a convenient way to have business meetings without traveling to other offices. On-screen conferencing enables several people to talk while seeing each other on screens via live internet. Besides saving time, it saves money since it cuts out the costs of travel and hotel stays. Talking via video is popular in nonbusiness groups such as families and friends too.

Videoconferencing

HOW DID SOCIAL MEDIA CHANGE THE WAY PEOPLE INTERACT?

The term "social media" refers to websites or apps that can be used to communicate socially or for work. Through popular social media platforms such as Twitter, Facebook, Instagram, and WhatsApp, we can share articles, photographs, videos, and audio messages with many people instantly. This wasn't possible with just phones and emails.

Social media apps on a smartphone

DOES BODY LANGUAGE REMAIN THE SAME IN ALL CULTURES?

No, various gestures and expressions differ widely in meaning from culture to culture. A handshake is interpreted differently in the Western world compared to the East. Curling the index finger to ask someone to come closer is considered rude in China. In the Middle Eastern countries, eye contact between men and women beyond a glance is considered inappropriate, while in most Western countries it is a sign of confidence.

Shaking hands

WHAT IS EMAIL?

Email is electronic mail. It is a method of sending and receiving messages by electronic communications systems such as computers and cell phones. The first email was sent in 1972. By 2020, a few hundred billion emails were being sent and received each day!

Email communication

Rapid-FIRE ?

WHAT IS A HOTLINE?

It is a direct phone line that will be answered immediately, often used for emergency services or to ask for help.

Hotline hub

HOW MANY PEOPLE USE CELL PHONES?

More than six billion people own cell phone subscriptions and the number of cell phones has already exceeded the human population!

Mobile phone

DOES SHAKING THE HEAD ALWAYS MEAN "NO"?

No, in some cultures it means "yes"!

HOW MANY LANGUAGES
ARE SPOKEN AROUND THE WORLD?

An estimated 7,000 languages are in use today across all countries. 20 of these languages are spoken by half of the world's people. The exact number of spoken languages is difficult to pin down since new findings about society and culture keep changing the total.

Rapid-FIRE?

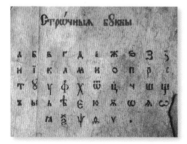

WHICH ALPHABET IS RUSSIAN WRITTEN IN?

The Cyrillic alphabet.

Ancient Cyrillic letters

WHICH ALPHABET ORIGINATED IN ANCIENT INDIA?

Devanagari—it's used for over 120 languages, including Hindi and Nepali.

Devanagari script

ON WHICH CONTINENT WOULD YOU HEAR SWAHILI?

Africa.

WHICH IS THE LEAST-SPOKEN LANGUAGE?

There are many languages that are rarely spoken, and most have no written form. Languages such as Ongota of Ethiopia, S'aoch of Cambodia, and Jarawa of the Andaman Islands have almost died out, with just a handful of speakers left.

ARE ALL ALPHABETS WRITTEN FROM LEFT TO RIGHT?

No, all alphabets are not the same and their style of writing can differ vastly. The Roman alphabet used for English is written (and read) left-to-right on the page but the Arabic language flows right-to-left. Traditional Japanese is written top-to-bottom.

Arabic script

Ancient Egyptian hieroglyphs etched in stone

Big? DO ALPHABETS DIFFER FROM LANGUAGE TO LANGUAGE?

Ancient Vietnamese books written with Chinese characters

Since the time humans started using pictures to express or record events, many cultures have developed a script to go with their spoken language. The Latin language's alphabet of 26 letters is the most widely used in the world. Hanzi, the Chinese script consisting of thousands of characters, dates back to 1200 BCE, and is the base for Chinese, Korean, and Japanese writing. The Arabic alphabet goes back to nearly 400 CE, and is the third most widely used, including for Persian, Urdu, Pashto, Punjabi, and many other languages.

CAN THERE BE ONE LANGUAGE FOR THE WHOLE WORLD?

A language called Esperanto was created in 1887 by Dr L.L. Zamenhof, a Polish linguist, with the intention that it would become an international second language for all. Esperanto is derived from the roots of European languages. Though it did not achieve widespread usage, more than 100,000 people do speak the language today.

Esperanto Alphabet

Aa	Bb	Cc	Ĉĉ	Dd	Ee	Ff	Gg	Ĝĝ	Hh
Hĥ	Ii	Jj	Ĵĵ	Kk	Ll	Mm	Nn	Oo	Pp
	Rr	Ss	Ŝŝ	Tt	Uu	Ŭŭ	Vv	Zz	

Written Esperanto

IS A SINGLE LANGUAGE SPOKEN IN ONE COUNTRY?

Mostly not. A country contains people of different cultures, tribes, ethnicities, and origins, who prefer to speak their own languages. For example, many cities worldwide have a Chinatown, where Chinese people live and speak English, and a variety of Chinese dialects. Even street signs are in both languages.

Street signage in two languages

A HEALTHY BODY

WHY DO WE GET SICK?

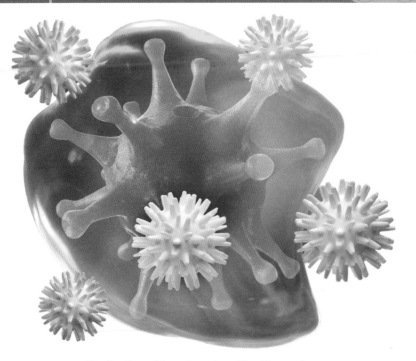

Illness is caused by either a failure of one of the body's functions or because microbes and germs invade our body. The human body has a defense system called the immune system that is capable of identifying germs. The body then fights the germs with special immune cells to become healthy again.

Illustration of lymphocytes attacking a virus

WHAT ARE INFECTIOUS AND NONINFECTIOUS DISEASES?

Any disease, like a cold, that can pass from one person to another is called infectious. These diseases are spread through dirty water or food, through the air, by touching the germ on a dirty surface, or even by mosquito bites. Noninfectious diseases, such as cancer and heart disease, are not passed from person to person.

Mosquito sucking blood

Big?

HOW DOES THE IMMUNE SYSTEM FIGHT DISEASE?

Virus

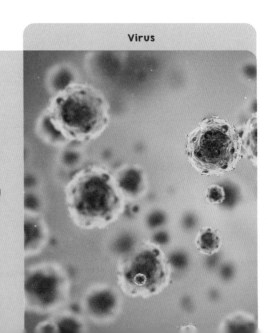

The immune system springs into action when germs such as bacteria, viruses, and fungi enter our body. Immune cells patrol throughout the blood, but are concentrated in the lymphatic system. When germs are detected, the immune system mounts a counterattack by flooding the blood with immune cells. You know that the immune system has been activated when you have a fever, weakness, and inflammation. Two types of immune cells are most important: B-lymphocytes, which attach antibodies to germs, and killer T-cells, which identify the targets with antibodies and swamp them.

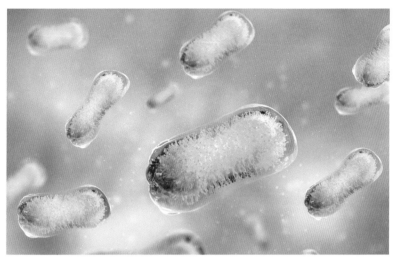

Microbes

WHAT IS "DISEASE"?

The word comes from Latin and means "absence of ease." Diseases are medical conditions that affect the body and have particular symptoms and signs. A disease could be due to an external cause, such as microbes and germs, or from an internal cause, such as a weak immune system or allergic reaction.

WHAT IS THE DIFFERENCE BETWEEN CHRONIC AND ACUTE DISEASE?

If a disease lasts for a long period of time, it is called chronic. It could be continuously present or may come and go from time to time. It can remain stable or worsen. An acute disease is short and sudden. Like a common cold, it can start suddenly but it goes away, or is cured in a short time.

Being sick with a cold

Rapid-FIRE ?

WHO IS THE "FATHER OF MEDICINE"?

Hippocrates, a brilliant Greek physician of the fourth and fifth centuries BCE.

Hippocrates

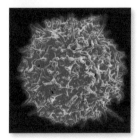

T-cell

Are T-CELLS GOOD WARRIORS

Yes. One T-cell can destroy up to 100 bacteria.

WHAT DOES "IDIOPATHY" MEAN?

A disease for which a cause has not been found.

WHAT IS A PLACEBO EFFECT?

A condition where a person feels better only because they believe that the treatment is working.

WHAT ARE MICROBES AND PATHOGENS?

Microbes are tiny organisms such as viruses and bacteria that exist everywhere, including in and on your body. Pathogens are those microbes that can cause disease. Not all microbes are harmful; in fact, many are beneficial to humans and the environment. Microbes can spread though skin contact, air, and fluids. Pathogens need to survive in a living body where they multiply, trying to get past our immune system and infect us.

WHAT ARE SOME COMMON BACTERIAL DISEASES?

The most deadly disease of the 20th century caused by bacteria was tuberculosis, or TB. The TB bacteria works by tricking our immune system into lowering its defenses. TB is now a rare disease. The other way bacteria cause disease is by releasing toxins in our body. Cholera, meningitis, and diphtheria are also bacterial diseases.

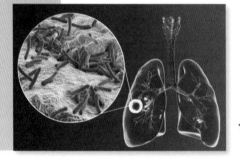

TB bacteria in the lungs

Rapid-FIRE ?

Mycobacterium leprae

Bifidobacteria

WHAT CAUSES LEPROSY?

A rod-shaped bacterium called *Mycobacterium leprae*.

IS THE BIFIDOBACTERIA GOOD FOR US?

Yes, it controls the growth of bad bacteria in our intestine.

CAN **ANTIBIOTIC MEDICINES KILL VIRUSES?**

No, they kill bacteria. Antiviral medicines are used to kill some viruses.

DO **VIRUSES HARM US AS SOON AS THEY ENTER OUR BODY?**

Many viruses can remain inactive for a long period inside us before they begin replicating.

Microbes seen under a microscope

HOW DO **VACCINES WORK?**

Vaccines are given to protect people and prevent them from catching a disease. Vaccines contain a version of a bacteria or virus that is dead or has been weakened. They are usually given to us in liquid form as injections and help our immune system learn how to recognize and fight the same viruses and bacteria when they try to infect us again.

WHAT IS THE
COVID-19 PANDEMIC?

COVID-19 is a type of coronavirus, a family of viruses that affects the respiratory system. A pandemic is when a disease spreads all over the world. The COVID-19 virus appeared in China in 2019 and it soon became a pandemic, infecting many millions of people.

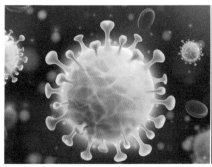

The COVID-19 coronavirus

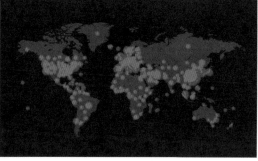

Spread of COVID-19

Big?
HOW DOES A **VIRUS INFECT US?**

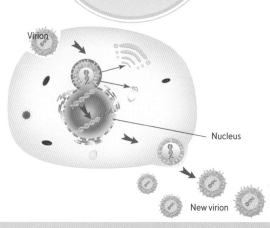

Virion

Nucleus

New virion

Virus replication

A virus enters the body through the mouth, nose, eyes, or cuts in the skin. Once inside the body, a virus injects its genetic material into a host cell. By hijacking the host cell the virus is able to make copies of itself. As the virus multiplies the host cell dies. The virus then moves into more cells. At this point, the body gets sick.

WHAT IS A MEDICAL DIAGNOSIS?

When a person is sick or injured, the doctor needs to know exactly what is wrong with the body before the treatment can begin. An unhealthy body has signs, called symptoms—a cough, a rash, a pain, and so on—which act like clues. This process of looking at the symptoms to find the cause of the illness or injury is known as diagnosis.

A doctor examining a patient

Big? WHAT ARE THE METHODS OF DIAGNOSIS?

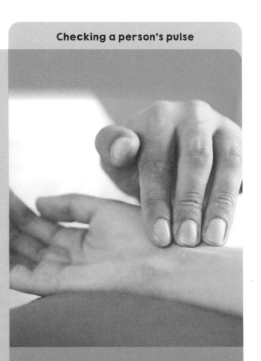

Checking a person's pulse

Diagnosis begins with the doctor asking questions about the symptoms that the patient is showing. The answers give clues to the cause of the disease. The doctor then looks at and listens to the relevant parts of the body, which helps pinpoint the exact problem. This is called a physical examination. It includes tapping the tummy, listening to the heartbeat, or checking the pulse rate and temperature. After that, the doctor may prescribe medication. If they are still not sure, they will ask for certain tests, such as of the blood and urine, as well as some scans. The results of all these allow the doctor to prescribe medication and predict the time needed for healing or recovery.

WHAT IS A STETHOSCOPE?

It is an instrument used to listen to the sounds inside the chest of the patient. A stethoscope has a flat disk that picks up sounds, and a tube that transmits them to the doctor's ears. It gives clues to problems connected with breathing and the heart.

Rapid-FIRE ?

WHAT IS AN OPHTHALMOSCOPE?

A device to check the eyes.

Ophthalmoscope

WHAT IS A SPHYGMOMANOMETER?

A blood-pressure monitor.

Sphygmomanometer

WHAT ARE X-RAYS?

X-rays take a black-and-white picture of the inside of our body. X-rays pass straight through certain tissues in our body, showing up as black on the photographic film. Tissues that block the path of the X-rays—often bones—show up white on film. X-rays are often taken to check for injuries to bones.

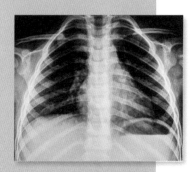

A chest X-ray

WHAT DOES A THERMOMETER MEASURE?

Body temperature. A clinical thermometer contains mercury, while a digital device uses a resistance temperature detector.

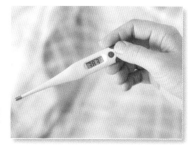

Digital thermometer

WHAT IS AN MRI?

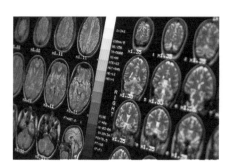

Magnetic resonance imaging (MRI) is a type of scan that uses strong magnetic fields and radio waves to produce detailed pictures of the inside of the body.

MRI-scan report

HOW DOES A CT-SCAN WORK?

CT, or computerized tomography, scans the body using computers. Inside a CT-scanner, a tube rotates around the patient, shooting X-rays as it goes. Light detectors on the opposite side pick up the rays. A computer builds up a detailed picture.

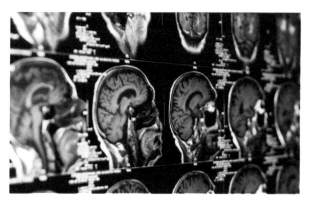

CT-scan report

Daily washing is an integral part of good personal hygiene.

WHAT IS HYGIENE?

To preserve health, we need to practice good hygiene. Taking a regular bath or shower, trimming nails, washing clothes, keeping our teeth and mouth clean are all essentials of personal hygiene. Hygiene also involves keeping our homes and surroundings clean.

WHAT IS IMMUNIZATION?

It is a process in which the body is vaccinated—injected with an inactive version of a germ. The body creates antibodies against the germ and becomes resistant or immune to infection in the future if attacked by an active version of the same germ.

Getting a vaccination

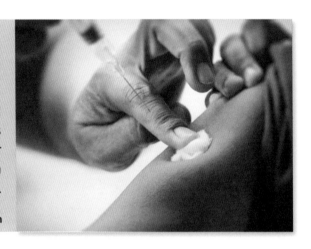

Rapid-FIRE?

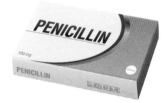

Penicillin

WHAT IS PENICILLIN?

An antibiotic, a class of drugs used to fight bacteria.

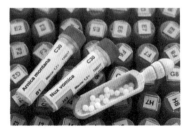

Homeopathic medicine

WHAT IS HOMEOPATHY?

It is a complementary therapy developed in Germany, based on the belief that the body, in time, can heal itself.

ARE THERE DIFFERENT TYPES OF IMMUNITY?

Yes. Active immunity develops when a person produces antibodies when exposed to a disease. Passive immunity takes place when a person receives antibodies, for example vaccination.

WHAT IS AIDS?

It stands for Acquired Immunodeficiency Syndrome, which is a viral disease. There is no cure but there are treatments to help a person fight it and remain healthy.

WHAT ARE ALTERNATIVE MEDICINES?

These are traditional methods of prevention and cure passed down from generation to generation over thousands of years. Some use herbs as treatment, such as in the Ayurveda system, in India. In China, a treatment called acupuncture involves inserting needles at selected points on the body to relieve illnesses.

Preparing herbal medicine

HOW HAS IMMUNIZATION HELPED?

Many previously common diseases like diphtheria, polio, measles, and whooping cough are now quite rare, all thanks to mass vaccination. Smallpox, a deadly disease, has been wiped out.

WHY DO WE GET HOSPITALIZED?

When we are sick, proper care is as important as the correct medicine. If we are mildly ill, our family and friends can take care of us at home and help with the right medicine and care. But if we are more seriously ill, we need nurses and doctors to monitor our body in the hospital and give us regular treatment.

A doctor checking on a patient in the hospital

Big? WHAT ARE MEDICINES?

The original penicillin mold

Many illnesses are treated with medicines. In the past, medicines mostly came from natural substances such as molds and fungi. Now they are made in laboratories with chemicals, and even designed on computers. A few medicines are made by manipulating genes of living organisms. The range of medicines now available is very wide. Most come in the form of pills to swallow. A few are injected directly into the blood with a needle. Some are available to buy over-the-counter from a pharmacy or other store; others have to be prescribed by a doctor.

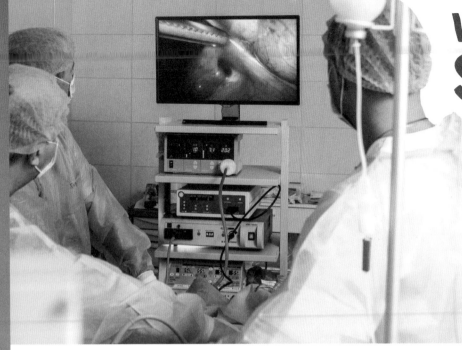

A laparoscopic surgery in progress

WHAT IS SURGERY?

In some situations, the only way to treat the body is to repair it physically, often by cutting into it to treat the affected area. This is called surgery. Surgeons are highly skilled doctors who can make these direct repairs, remove a diseased part of the body, or mend a broken bone.

CAN MISSING LIMBS BE REPLACED?

If a person has lost an arm or leg due to an accident, injury, or perhaps they were born without it, they may be able to get a replacement. Prosthetics are artificial parts attached to the body. Artificial limbs can be very advanced and restore the function of that part of the body.

Man with a prosthetic leg

Big **?** CAN THE BODY'S ORGANS BE REPLACED?

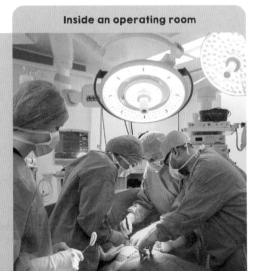

Inside an operating room

Sometimes, when an organ can no longer perform its function and the body gets very sick, a doctor may remove the diseased part and replace it with a healthy organ. Many vital organs such as the heart, kidney, liver, lungs, pancreas, and cornea of the eye can be transplanted by surgeons. The replacement organ is given by a donor. Transplant operations can be complex, but are usually lifesaving.

WHAT IS A **PACEMAKER?**

When people suffer from heart problems, a tiny electronic device can sometimes be implanted into the chest, and small wires connected to the heart. It sends out electrical signals to the heart muscles to keep the heart beating steadily. This device is called a pacemaker. It is used to regulate or replace the heart's electrical conduction system.

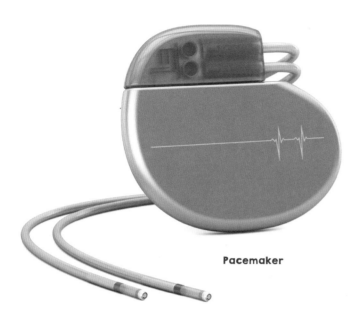

Pacemaker

HOW IS **SURGERY DONE WITHOUT CAUSING PAIN?**

Before an operation, a drug is applied or injected to numb the area so that the body can be operated on. This drug is called an anesthetic, and it can be general or local. A general anesthetic makes a patient unconscious (like being asleep) during the whole operation so he or she has no awareness or feeling for what is happening. In a local anesthetic, only that part of the body that is being operated on is numb.

WHAT ARE **IMPLANTS?**

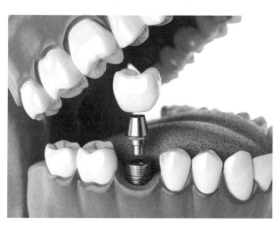

A tooth implant

At times, damaged or worn body parts, such as the hip bone or knees, are replaced with similar parts specially made of materials like titanium, ceramic, and plastic. This process is called an implant. The artificial parts are surgically inserted and placed inside the body.

Rapid-FIRE **?**

WHAT IS A **LAPAROSCOPY?**

A type of surgery that uses a thin tube to send a tiny camera inside your body. It shows the doctors what is making you sick and allows them to fix it, without making any more than a tiny cut.

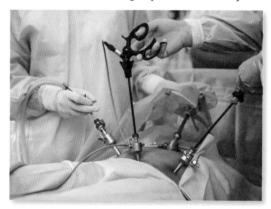

Laparoscopy

HOW IS **ROBOTIC SURGERY PERFORMED?**

With tiny tools attached to robotic arms controlled by surgeons through a computer.

Robotic surgery

CAN WE LIVE A NORMAL LIFE WITH ONLY **ONE KIDNEY?**

Yes.

WHY EXERCISE?

Physical exercise is activity to develop and maintain body fitness. It has many benefits: it makes us strong, agile, flexible, and energetic; it keeps our heart and lungs in good shape; and it helps prevent disease and improves our quality of life. For the greatest benefits, we need to make physical exercise part of our regular routine.

Exercise can be fun!

WHAT IS RESISTANCE TRAINING?

Strength and resistance training strengthen our muscles, ligaments, and joints. It involves working our muscles against some sort of resistance, like weights, gym machines, exercise bands, or just our own body weight.

Big? DOES EXERCISE HELP US GROW?

Yes, it does: it improves both our physical and mental health. Physical activity, such as playing games, skipping, catching a ball, skating, cycling, swinging, and climbing, is particularly important for children. It not only develops strong bones, muscle strength, flexibility, and stamina, but also increases brain activity and alertness. It helps build a smooth connection between the brain and nerves, which helps improves hand-eye coordination and motor skills and gives us greater control over our bodies.

Playing jump rope

IS **SWIMMING GOOD EXERCISE?**

Yes. Going for a swim is an excellent way to work all the muscles of the body and build up stamina with little risk of injuring bones and joints. Having to control breathing also strengthens the heart and lungs.

Enjoying a swim

HOW MUCH **PHYSICAL ACTIVITY DO WE NEED?**

It depends on the type of exercise and what we want to achieve. Regular physical activity keeps us healthy and strong. Children should have at least 60 minutes of moderate-intensity activity every day, while adults need a minimum of 20 minutes.

Running is good exercise

ARE THERE EXERCISES THAT **HELP IMPROVE YOUR BALANCE?**

Our movements, while turning around, climbing stairs, skating, playing soccer and so on, naturally involve a lot of balancing. Sometimes it is necessary to improve balance and coordination to become better at a favorite sport, such as gymnastics. For older people, good balance can prevent them from falling and getting injured. Tai chi is particularly good for balance.

Rapid-FIRE **?**

IS **DANCING AN EXERCISE?**

Yes, it builds balance, cardiovascular fitness, and agility.

Dance as exercise

IS **DRINKING WATER IMPORTANT AFTER EXERCISE?**

Yes—lots of water is needed to replace what was sweated out.

Drinking regularly

HOW DO YOU **REDUCE THE CHANCES OF INJURY WHILE EXERCISING?**

By warming up, stretching, and cooling down.

Stretching

WHAT IS **YOGA GOOD FOR?**

Whole-body flexibility, fitness, and control.

WHAT IS A BALANCED DIET?

The human body receives its energy from the food that we eat. This food is mostly one of three types—carbohydrates, fats, and proteins. Besides these, the body also needs vitamins and minerals. A balanced diet consists of healthy meals that include all the types of food required in the right proportion and quantity.

High-fiber foods

Big **?** WHAT SHOULD WE EAT FOR OUR BODY TO STAY HEALTHY?

Carbohydrates

Proteins

Nuts, beans, and seeds

Fats

A balanced diet keeps the body healthy

Rice and bread in our meals are sources of carbohydrates. Oil or butter in our cooking provide fat. And meat, fish, and eggs are mainly protein. Nuts, seeds, and beans are also rich in protein. A good diet needs the correct amounts of carbohydrates, proteins, and fats, and includes generous portions of fresh fruits and vegetables. Too many carbohydrates—more than we burn through exercise and physical activity—are stored as fat. Too much fat can make the heart unhealthy.

WHY DO WE NEED FIBER IN OUR DIET?

Fiber is basically the indigestible part of food that comes from plants. Fruit, vegetables, grains, beans, and legumes contain fiber. A good diet is necessary to keep the digestive system healthy.

WHAT ARE **VITAMINS?**

These are 13 major chemicals vital for our body to function. They are Vitamin A, C, D, E, K, and eight types of Vitamin B. We only need them in small quantities but they are absolutely necessary since they take care of a range of tasks in our body.

Foods rich in vitamins

Rapid-FIRE ?

WHAT ARE "EMPTY CALORIES"?

Sugar, fat, or oil in cookies, soft drinks, and other junk food provide energy but no nutrition. That's why they are called "empty calories."

"Junk" food

WHY IS BREAKFAST IMPORTANT?

Breakfast, as the first meal of the day, gives us the nutrients to maintain our energy throughout the day.

Healthy breakfast

WHAT ARE CALORIES IN FOOD?

Calories are a way of measuring the amount of energy that we get from food.

WHAT ARE ESSENTIAL MINERALS?

There are over a dozen. Among them are salt, calcium, iron, and tiny traces of iodine. They help to build strong bones and teeth.

ARE FATS BAD FOR OUR BODY?

No, fats are needed by the body as energy reserves. Fats are also an excellent source of Vitamins D and E, both necessary to keep our bones and skin healthy. It is only when fats are eaten in too great a quantity that they are bad for us.

Eggs contain all nine essential amino acids.

WHAT ARE THE ESSENTIAL AMINO ACIDS?

The body needs 21 amino acids for healthy body function. Nine amino acids, called essential amino acids, cannot be made by the body so must come from the diet. The remaining 12 amino acids are produced by the body.

WHAT DOES A DIETITIAN DO?

A dietitian is a qualified health professional who provides advice on what foods we should eat to stay healthy. Dietitians also provide eating plans for patients suffering from medical conditions, such as diabetes. These nutrition experts provide practical dietary advice to help improve a patient's symptoms and quality of life.

A dietitian understands the food your body needs.

Big? WHAT IS DIETING?

Establishing healthy food habits

Dieting is a process by which we might limit ourselves to certain foods to either gain, lose or maintain weight. To lose weight, we might lower our daily calorie intake, and avoid heavily processed foods like certain snacks, breads, sugary drinks, and desserts. On the other hand, to gain weight, we might up our calorie intake, while also prioritizing nutrient dense foods. Whatever our goal, it's important to strike a healthy balance of protein, carbohydrates, and fats.

IS THERE AN IDEAL BODY WEIGHT?

No, human body types differ and so does the best body weight for each person. Weight depends on height, bone density, activity levels, and other factors. There is no universal best body weight. When we eat healthily and remain active by doing regular exercise, our body gradually attains a body weight at which we feel happy.

So many body types

IS **OLIVE OIL** GOOD FOR US?

Yes, olive oil has many benefits. It soothes inflammation, deters harmful microbes, and contains antioxidants for our cells. As part of a nutritious diet, olive oil helps prevent heart disease, obesity, and arthritis. Considered a healthy diet, the Mediterranean diet is high in unsaturated fats, such as olive oil.

Olive oil

WHAT ARE **SUPERFOODS?**

Some foods contain so much goodness that they are called superfoods. Berries, leafy greens, and cruciferous vegetables are examples of superfoods that can help us maintain our weight, fight disease, and live a long, healthy life. In their natural state, superfoods are mostly plant based, and rich in vitamins, minerals, and antioxidants, which protect our cells.

Superfood smoothie

Rapid-FIRE?

WHAT ARE **GOJI BERRIES?**

Bright red fruit that grow on shrubs originally found in Asia. Goji berries are loaded with antioxidants.

Fresh goji berries

IS **COFFEE HEALTHY?**

Coffee does have health benefits, but too much of it can upset digestion.

Coffee break

IS **CHOCOLATE GOOD FOR US?**

Dark chocolate in moderate amounts is thought to be good for the heart and health.

Dark chocolate

WHAT DO WE **GET FROM CHEESE?**

Calcium, fat, protein, and vitamins.

Cheese

WHAT IS A **VEGAN DIET?**

One that avoids all food from animals, including milk products such as cheese and butter.

DOES WHAT PEOPLE EAT DIFFER AROUND THE WORLD?

The food people eat depends on what is readily available in their area. Climatic factors affect the types of fruits and vegetables grown, with some plants preferring warm, sunny weather. Beliefs and traditions also influence the food people eat. For example, vegetarians avoid eating meat and fish, while vegans do not eat any animal products including milk or eggs.

A seafood dish

WHO MAKES THE WORLD'S HOTTEST CURRIES?

The people of India love eating hot, spicy curry, especially in southern India. Spices such as red and green chilies, pepper, ginger, garlic, turmeric, curry leaves, and many others go into the making of tasty curries.

Preparing curry paste

Rapid-FIRE ?

Paella

WHAT IS PAELLA?

A Spanish rice dish, with vegetables, meat, or seafood, and herbs, cooked slowly on an open fire.

Hummus

WHAT IS HUMMUS?

A spread used in the Middle East made of chickpeas, garlic, lemon juice, and tahini.

A tofu preparation

IS STINKY TOFU REALLY STINKY?

Yes. It is fermented in fermented milk and old brine.

WHO EATS THE MOST CHEESE?

Cheese is more popular in cold countries where it can be easily produced and preserved. Denmark, Iceland, Finland, and France all consume a lot of cheese. But it is the average Greek who consumes the most: almost 50 lbs every year! Three-quarters of this is feta cheese, made from sheep and goat milk.

Big? HOW DO WE KEEP FOOD FROM GOING BAD?

Different kinds of pickles

Refrigerators were the most important invention for food preservation. They were first used in 1876 to transport fresh beef from Argentina. Some other common methods used around the world to ensure foods remain edible are pickling, smoking, and drying. Preserved vegetables and meat pickles survive months without decay. Chutneys in India, miso in Japan, and salsas in Mexico are all different forms of preservation that prolongs the life of food. Preserving agents, called food additives, both natural and artificial, are used to extend the shelf life of foods. Pasteurization and sterilization both preserve foods by heating them to remove living organisms.

WHERE CAN YOU BUY MILK BY WEIGHT?

In the Russian Arctic, where temperatures fall below -104 °F, milk freezes. Yakutian cattle are special Russian cows adapted to the extreme cold and to survive on limited feed. They produce very rich milk that is sold in chunks weighed in gallons instead of volumes measured in liters.

Yakutian cow

WHAT IS THE NATIONAL DISH OF SCOTLAND?

Haggis, neeps, and tatties

Haggis. It is a savory dish of minced meat with oatmeal, onions, suet, seasoning, and spices, wrapped in a sheep's stomach, then boiled and eaten with neeps (mashed turnip) and tatties (mashed potatoes).

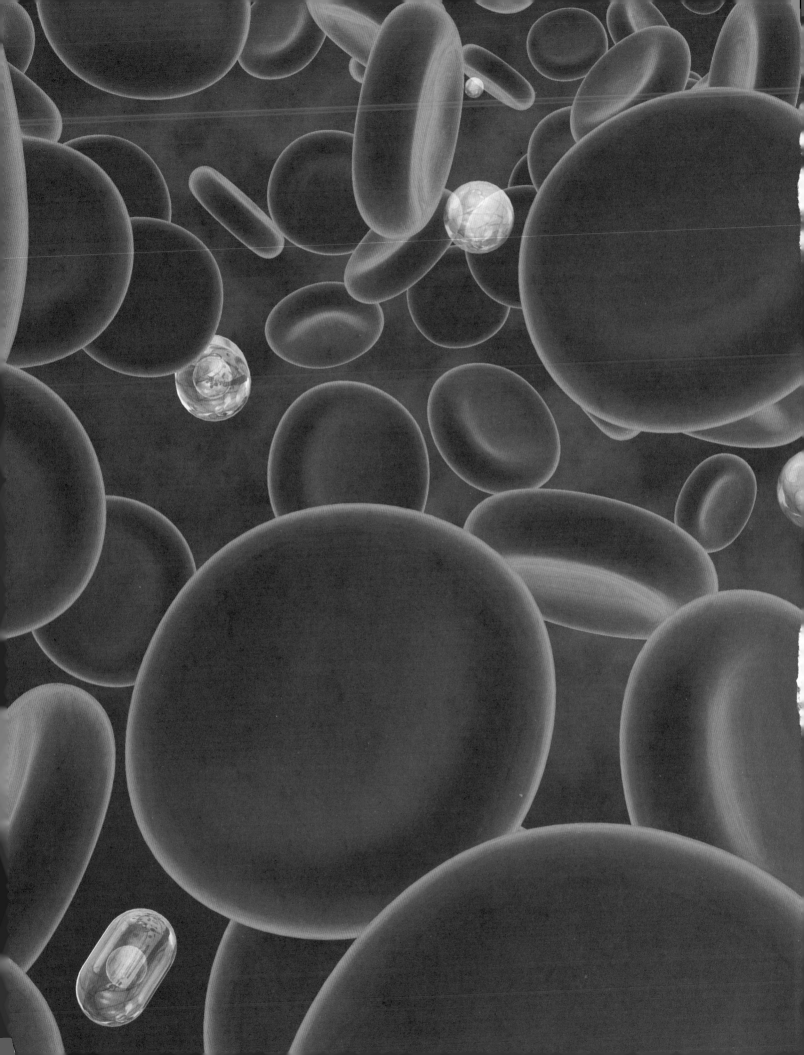